Veiling Architecture

Veiling Architecture

Decoration of Domestic Buildings in Upper Egypt, 1672–1950

Ahmed Abdel-Gawad

The American University in Cairo Press
Cairo • New York

Dar el Kutub No. 24574/11
ISBN 978 977 416 487 3

Dar el Kutub Cataloging-in-Publication Data

Abdel-Gawad, Ahmed
    Veiling Architecture: Decoration of Domestic Buildings in Upper Egypt 1672–1950/
    Ahmed Abdel-Gawad.—Cairo: The American University in Cairo Press, 2012
        p.   cm.
        ISBN 978 977 416 487 3
        1. Decoration and ornament—Egypt
        729.0962

1 2 3 4 5 6   14 13 12 11 12

Designed by Sally Boylan
Printed in Egypt

CONTENTS

ACKNOWLEDGMENTS

It gives me pleasure to thank the many people who helped me with this work. It would not have come to light without the helpful advice of Neil Hewison, associate director for editorial programs at the American University in Cairo Press. My affectionate thanks go to Habiba Mohamed Ali for her support and encouragement. I am also grateful to Mohamed Ali for his helpful assistance. My extended thanks also go to Abdalla F. Hassan, Nadia Naqib, and Anne Fikry, for their assistance and guidance.

Lastly, I would like to express my sincere gratitude to my wife for her support and help.

PREFACE

Very little has been written about the architecture of Upper (Southern) Egyptian residential buildings and their façades. The examples chosen for this book show several buildings from various towns, both large and small, which date from the late nineteenth to the first half of the twentieth century. This period witnessed the predominance of two architectural trends, which were imported during the periods of Muhammad ʿAli and Khedive Ismail, namely the Rumi and European styles. The building façades of this period were built in such a way as to express the imitation of and interaction between these two architectural trends and the more traditional Egyptian architectural styles of Upper Egyptian towns. This imitation and interaction was greatly influenced by the prevailing culture of these towns, which in turn stemmed largely from the rules of Islamic jurisprudence (*fiqh*).

The buildings featured in this book are selected from nineteen Upper Egyptian towns representing six governorates, which, extending from north to south, are: Beni Suef, Minya, Asyut, Sohag, Qena, and al-Wadi al-Gidid. The towns include Mallawi and Bahnasa (Minya Governorate); Manfalut, Dayrut al-Mahatta, and Dayrut al-Sharif (Asyut Governorate); Tima, Tahta, al-Maragha, and Girga (Sohag Governorate); Nagʿ Hammadi, Qift, and Qus (Qena Governorate); and al-Qasr and Dakhla Oasis (al-Wadi al-Gidid Governorate).

The first part of this study looks at neo-Islamic architecture and its modified types of mashrabiya (see page 3) and their decorations as well as the types of screens used for balconies, particularly the pierced-wood screens of local architecture.

The second part explores the shapes of end treatments of the top stories of buildings, executed in both local and eclectic styles. It also focuses on the shapes of pediment and stucco decorations.

The third part of this study provides a brief historical account of reception units since the Ottoman period, beginning in the nineteenth century and continuing until the first half of the twentieth century with the emergence of two-doorway local-style buildings. It also discusses and characterizes the four categories of doorway found in these towns, namely Rumi, European, the local style in Nile Valley towns, and the old-style doorways in the town of al-Qasr, which date back to the seventeenth century.

The six appendices of computer-assisted drawings bring together characteristic motifs of decoration found on different parts of the buildings examined in this book. These include wooden friezes of mashrabiya eaves, wooden screens, wooden ornamentation, pediments and rooflines, fanlights and upper parts of doorways, and lastly, lintels.

A note on the illustrations in this book: The plates in the Plates section are numbered by building. The computer-assisted drawings in the same section carry the labels ascribed to them in the appendices. For example, A14 is drawing number 14 in Appendix A ("Wooden Friezes of Mashrabiya Eaves").

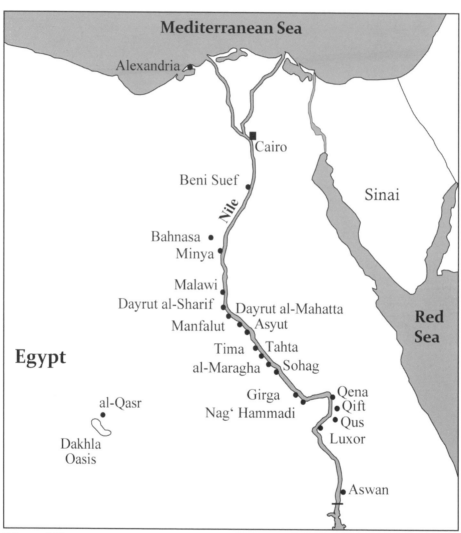

Map of Egypt

INTRODUCTION

The Architecture and Decoration
of the Houses of Upper Egypt

Houses of the Nile Valley Towns
from the Late Nineteenth to the Mid-Twentieth Century

Two main architectural trends have had a great impact on the Egyptian architectural tradition since the nineteenth century. The first trend is the Rumi style, adopted during the period of Muhammad 'Ali Pasha (1805–49). The second is the European style, adopted during the period of Khedive Ismail (1863–79).

During the last two decades of the nineteenth century and the first half of the twentieth, the residential architecture of the middle and upper classes in towns in the southern part of the Nile Valley was greatly influenced by these two waves of imported architecture. Nonetheless there were huge differences between large and small towns as to whether they completely imitated a style or created their own eclectic styles. Generally speaking, the large capitals of governorates, such as Beni Suef, Minya, Asyut, Sohag, and Qena, had greater capabilities than small towns like Dayrut, Tima, Tahta, or Girga in terms of architects, builders, craftsmen, as well as clients, to follow a particular style of architecture. Thus, large towns have good examples of imitations of the prototypes of architectural styles, such as the Rumi style. Nevertheless, small towns also have a few examples. There is a good imitation of an Art Nouveau villa, belonging to Fakhry Abdel Nour's famous family, built in 1910, in Girga (Qena Governorate). Mallawi (Minya

Governorate) also has a good imitation of a neo-Renaissance-style palace, built in AH 1325/1907 CE,[1] and belonging to Hayat al-Nufus, wife of Amin Tuni Bey, the mayor of Mallawi.

The Neo-Islamic-Style Houses in Upper Egyptian Towns

The two waves of imported architectural styles, the Rumi and the European, although greatly distracting from and excluding the principles and designs of the Egyptian architectural tradition, nevertheless helped to create other styles, such as neo-Islamic architecture, which was adopted wholeheartedly by both architects and clients.

The architectural styles popular in Cairo in the period 1863–1914 "were neoclassical, neo-Baroque, Art Nouveau, neo-Islamic, Mediterranean, and Eclectic styles."[2] Nevertheless, the decorative motifs and details changed from one style to another, as though the buildings were being customized in different styles according to the wishes and desires of the architect or client in question.[3]

The Rumi and European styles slowly but surely found their way into the old districts of Cairo, and were gradually adapted to existing architectural structures. Although the neo-Islamic style with its three classifications[4] had taken hold in most of the public buildings of the modern district in Cairo—realized by some architects returning from structural design missions in Europe—residential buildings in the old district of Cairo developed their own neo-Islamic style in parallel. In both districts, architects had been influenced by European designs and the principles predominant in its morphology, "that is, axiality in entrance and form, symmetry and regularity."[5] Thus, "the Islamic elements were applied to give the building an Islamic spirit."[6]

The adoption of Islamic elements differed greatly, in functional terms, between the two districts of Cairo. In the modern district, the Cairo of Khedive Ismail, "the style used primarily employed traditional decorative motifs,"[7] either in the portal block, or in the perforations (any opening in the façades and their architectural treatment, and decorative motifs such as fenestration, windows, balconies, and mashrabiyas), or in the cornices and end treatments (the architecture and decorative treatment of the part of a façade that projects from the top story, usually in the form of trefoil and stepped crestings). The style of the old district of Cairo, however, continued to use the mashrabiya as its main unit of perforation, with the employment of traditional decorative motifs in various parts of the building. This stemmed essentially from an observance of religious law, with its injunction to "avoid the detriment of unveiling" *(darar al-kashf),* particularly when the buildings in question were constructed in the narrow roads and alleyways of the old city.

The revival of the neo-Islamic style in old Cairo during the first three decades of the twentieth century was characterized by a close adherence to the Art Nouveau style, while the neo-Islamic style in the modern district was characterized by adherence to the neoclassical style.[8] The Art Nouveau style usually consisted "of three-story buildings having five-sided salient window bays in the middle, which were flanked by two corner bays of separate balconies with balustrades of worked iron."[9] Receptivity to this architectural style drew from its symmetrical appearance, rendering it convenient to small plot divisions, whether square or rectangular, overlooking the narrow streets and lanes of old Cairo.

As a result of this combination of Islamic elements and the Art Nouveau style, the neo-Islamic style in old Cairo developed two main prototypes. The first type was influenced by the characteristic bays of the Art Nouveau style, featuring a projecting central bay supported by brackets, with a vertically repeated mashrabiya. The projected bay was flanked by a recession on either side, which contained windows or balconies (figure 1).[10] The other prototype consisted of two- or three-story buildings that had a separate type of mashrabiya distributed either vertically or horizontally (figure 2).[11] In both prototypes the mashrabiya was modified and covered by lattice or shutter windows (figures 1 and 2),[12] or a combination of the two, instead of the small openings of turned wood, as had been popular in eighteenth-century mashrabiyas. The base of this type of modified mashrabiya took the form of wooden sheet panels, on which it was easy to create floral

Figure 1. Early twentieth-century architecture in old Cairo: example
of projected central bay, flanked on either side by a recession.

and geometric ornamentations. Usually, the top of the mashrabiya has a
wooden eave, while its base is surrounded by a wooden frieze;[13] both eave
and frieze are decorated by various Islamic motifs.

During the first three decades of the twentieth century one could discern
a diffusion of the neo-Islamic style, with its two prototypes, in both large
and small towns of Upper Egypt. It is difficult to say whether the neo-
Islamic style that had been developed in the towns of Upper Egypt was a
direct imitation of the prototype of the style then popular in the districts of
old Cairo, or if it had emerged spontaneously from the mind of an architect
subject to similar socioeconomic circumstances and from the same traditional cultural background as his or her Cairene counterparts.

Figure 2. Early twentieth-century architecture in old Cairo: example of separate, repeating mashrabiyas.

The Role Played by *Fiqh* in Architecture and the Rules of Decoration

The purpose of *fiqh* (Islamic jurisprudence) was to organize all economic, political, and social activities within Islamic society. It also regulated the rules of the construction of roads and their usage, markets and marketplaces, as well as the construction and decoration of residential buildings.

In Islamic society the word for 'dwelling,' *sakan*, is associated with calm, meaning silence and tranquillity *(sakina)*, and most important of all is the privacy of the occupants of that dwelling. In the eighteenth century, the observance of such privacy was the most important condition of a residence's architectural makeup. Hence violation of this privacy was a matter one sought to avoid, since it could result in "the detriment of disclosure," that is, exposing the private lives of the residents of those dwellings, and their dealings with relatives and visitors. The jurisprudential rule *la darar wa la dirar* ('neither mischief nor reciprocal harm'), that is, a Muslim does not harm his Muslim brother, sought to regulate conduct for the purpose of protecting residents' privacy, thus establishing a law of conduct in the field of building construction that became a tradition adhered to by all the members of Islamic communities, and therefore both house owners and house builders alike. The law of conduct in construction lays out several points that deal with architecture and decoration units. These include (1) the shape and location of perforations; (2) the location of portal units; and (3) the shape of the buildings' end treatments.

The Modified Mashrabiya in the Houses of Upper Egyptian Towns

The commitment to the jurisprudential rule that aimed to avoid "the detriment of unveiling" had a great influence on the shape and decoration of the façade perforations of Islamic residential buildings. The main impact was twofold. First, it led to the screening of building perforations with turned-wood work, either in a mashrabiya as a projecting unit in the façade, or in windows that are level with the façade. Second, it led to the emergence of a rule by which it is prohibited to open one's perforation just in front of a neighbor's opening, as Ibn al-Rami (AH 618/1258 CE) noted.[14]

The mashrabiya is considered one of the most traditional elements of Islamic architecture, still clearly discernble in the residential buildings of Upper Egyptian towns. Besides playing a decorative role, it continued to fulfill its traditional functions, namely that of regulating air movement, controlling light quantity, and enabling residents to retain contact with the outside world, while preserving their privacy.

Mashrabiyas in a house situated in Grand Mosque Street in Qena represent the first prototype of the neo-Islamic style (plate 1a). The house's façade has a projecting central bay with two recesses containing separate balconies. The central bay has two vertically repeated mashrabiyas. The base of the mashrabiyas constitutes a height of one-third of the mashra-biya's total height, while the top level constitutes a height of two-thirds. The latter part contains two big shutter windows with double wooden leaves on the outside and double glass leaves on the inside. The leaves of the external wooden window are divided into two parts: the lower part makes up about two-thirds of the window's height while the upper part constitutes a third. The bigger, lower parts of the window leaves can be closed, leaving the small upper parts open, and vice versa. In this way the traditional functions of the mashrabiya are clearly fulfilled. It is worth noting here that the wooden panels at the base of the mashrabiya contain different types of projecting wooden work, which are fixed to the base with glue and nails (plate 1b).

The house next door to the one just described (plate 5a) is an example of the traditional and separate type of eighteenth-century mashrabiya. It is made of three types of lathe-turned wood that are dovetailed into each other. This mashrabiya also has a new feature, a narrow area in its center, con-taining small louvered shutters with modern horizontal slats.

Decreasing the size of the mashrabiya's movable units directly increases the speed of air current, leading to good ventilation and a cooler indoor atmosphere.[15] This system can be seen in the mashrabiya of a house situ-ated in Bahari al-Balad Street in Qena (plate 6b). This type of mashrabiya consists completely of wooden shutters made up of horizontally angled slats. The upper and lower parts take the shape of fixed window frames for the sole purpose of decoration, while the middle third takes the shape of small windows, which can be opened. Their leaves have a width of about twenty centimeters. This small size allows for the freedom of open-ing them without violation of the four traditional functions of the mashrabiya (ensuring privacy, regulating air movement, controlling sun-light, allowing residents to stay in touch with the outside world). In a house located in al-Markaz Street in Qena (plate 8), there is another type of this modified mashrabiya, one divided into a lower third consisting of panels without decorations, and topped by an upper part that makes up about two thirds of the mashrabiya's total height. This part consists of double-leaf lattice windows, three in the front, and two at each side. These windows are at two levels: large windows are at a low level and small windows about half their height are above them. The existence of windows at two levels (upper and lower), and the multiplicity of the functions of these windows, both large and small, is regarded as a creative means of accomplishing the traditional functions of the mashrabiya. The technique of dividing large windows into small ones, and also that of distributing these openings between the front and two sides, is typical of this type of mashrabiya.

The closed type of mashrabiya of Minya is characterized by two features: the material used for its screening, and its outer shape. The mashrabiya is divided vertically into three equal longitudinal parts demarcated by four wooden columns with spiral decoration. Horizontally, each part is divided into four levels. The base is formed of wooden panels, which usually have star-plated ornamentation executed by means of projecting wooden strips fixed by glue and nails. The second level is screened by double-leaf glass windows; the third level is screened by geometric wooden-framed glass; and the top level takes the shape of trefoiled or semicircular wooden tracery (plates 14a and 14b). Usually the top of the mashrabiya has a wooden eave decorated by small crestings, in an inverted or straight position (A23).

Open Mashrabiya

Besides the closed mashrabiya, which is screened by lattice and louvered shutters (as in the house in Qena), or by glass windows (as in Minya), yet another type of mashrabiya has appeared, namely one that does not completely close. Thus we can make a distinction between two types of open mashrabiya. The first type is to be found in Qena, the second in Minya.

Open Mashrabiya with Columns in Qena

Many examples of the open mashrabiya are found in Qena. The lower part of this type of mashrabiya, which is about half the total height, seems completely closed, but the upper part can be opened. There are round columns with large diameters of about 0.15–0.20 meters at each corner of the mashrabiya. There may exist a third column either in front or in the center of the mashrabiya. These columns end in arches that carry the mashrabiya's wooden roof. The top of this mashrabiya is encircled with projecting eaves decorated with wooden crestings.

In the mashrabiya of a house in Grand Mosque Street in Qena (plate 12a) we can see that the closed lower half is, in turn, divided into a lower part; about two thirds of its height is covered with wooden sheet panels, and the upper third consists of a row of louvered shutters that open to the sides. The form of these shutters, apart from their small size, reflects yet another method of controlling vision: by way of wooden slats, which move up or down while the shutters are closed. Each shutter has about ten slats, which are fixed to each other by a longitudinal wooden hand in the middle, and their ends are fixed to the edges of the shutters' stiles. They are slightly angled to admit air and light, and can be moved freely. Pushing the wooden hand down turns the ten slats to a horizontal position; the spaces between them become larger, thus widening the area of vision and allowing a clearer view onto the road. When the hand is moved up, the slats go back to their normal inclined position, and the area of vision becomes narrow again, making it difficult for passersby to see the inhabitants behind the mashrabiya. So there are two ways to make vision through these shutters possible—by opening them, or by moving a set of slats up and down while the shutters themselves stay closed.

It is worth noting that this mashrabiya has three columns; these columns end in two shallow arches that carry the wooden roof of the mashrabiya. In other examples of these types of mashrabiya we observe just two columns (plate 13a).

Upper Narrow-opening Mashrabiya in Minya

In Minya the second type of open mashrabiya is common. In this mashrabiya a narrow area between the topmost level of the lower part and the upper edge of the mashrabiya is left open. Hence this type of mashrabiya consists of three distinguishable parts: the lower part, the narrow opening, and the upper-part-like cover.

The lower part constitutes three-quarters to four-fifths of the total height of the mashrabiya, which measures 1.9–2.1 meters on average. The base of the lower part consists of panels in different shapes, decorated by various star-plate motifs. The center of the lower part, which represents the area of vision, is screened by shutter windows of different sizes (plates 18b, 19b, and 20b). This part may be screened by movable panels of pierced wood (plate 22b).

The second part, which makes up between one-fifth and one-quarter of the total height of the mashrabiya, facilitates another method of ventilation, especially designed for this type of mashrabiya. The air current coming from outside enters this open area at high speed. It then moves downward to the lower levels of the house, thus acting like a continuous air stream, which constantly refreshes the air within the house.

The third part of this type of mashrabiya is partially screened to minimize its total size. In some examples this screen may take the shape of two pierced, shallow arches, each opposing a pierced, projecting semicircular shape (plates 19b and 22b). Sometimes the screen takes the shape of a shallow arch containing plant-shape motifs in its corners (plate 20b). In other examples this part is covered by glass sheet panes, which can be closed as a means of protection against dust storms during the *khamasin* season (plate 22a and 23b).

The Emergence of Eclectic-style Houses in Upper Egyptian Towns

Large-scale buildings belonging to wealthy people in the towns of Upper Egypt were erected according to a specially developed style. Some of these buildings imitated the structure and morphology of the Rumi-style architecture as seen in the towns of Beni Suef (plate 69), while others only imitated the Rumi-style doorways, as seen in Sohag (plates 35b and 70).

During the first three decades of the twentieth century a number of these large-scale buildings acquired some of the characteristics of European-style architecture, and in the end vaguely took on their own particular style. One of these characteristics took the form of the recesses in the Eclectic style with its gallery balconies.[16] These buildings developed their own projections, which did not follow any particular style. The projections also had gallery balconies. So these large-scale buildings had two types of gallery balconies—recessed (plates 35a, 43, and 50b) or projected (plate 42a).

Besides the two prototypes of gallery balconies in large-scale buildings, small-scale and low-income houses had the usual projected balconies. According to the rule of "avoiding the detriment of unveiling and respecting privacy," these two types of balconies (gallery and usual) were screened by pierced wood, reflecting the very special motives behind the ornamentation prevailing in Upper Egyptian towns. Screening of both types of balconies (which usually had a height of 1.1 to 1.3 meters) could be seen in large-, medium-, and small-scale houses. Wooden balustrades could be seen in the southern and eastern terrace of the Hayat al-Nufus Palace in Mallawi (plate 24). An area of vision including small lattice or shutter windows might be added to the top level of the balustrade (which increased its total length to 1.5–1.8 meters) and could be seen in wealthy family homes, as in the balcony of the Qurashi family house (plate 57) in Dayrut al-Mahatta (Asyut Governorate), or in medium-scale houses as in Qena (plate 51).

In the Khashaba Pasha Family's house, located in Port Said Street in Asyut, the gallery balcony projects 0.5 meters beyond the façade. The lower two-thirds of the balustrade are made of pierced wood while the upper third takes the form of a cornice of lattice wood (plate 46b). A gallery balcony can be seen in the house of Dayrut al-Sharif (plate 44b). The balcony is projected 0.8 meters beyond the façade. The lower part of the screen of pierced wood is topped by an area of vision of five small shutter-openings, three in front and two at each side.

In Sohag, the gallery balcony overlooks the corner of al-Corniche and al-Qaffas streets and has a 0.5-meter projection from the façade. It has a wooden eave supported by four wooden columns. The two balconies overlooking al-Corniche Street are of a recessed type, with balustrades 1.1–1.3 meters high. While the balustrade of the first balcony is divided into two halves—a lower half made of solid wood and an upper half of pierced wood—the balustrade of the second balcony, which is shorter in height than that of the first balcony, is completely screened by pierced wood. This system of screening allows for a gradual coverage in respect of the principle of ensuring privacy, varying between the first balcony, which is close to the road, and the second balcony, which is at a distance from the road.

Wooden-Screen Technique

The wooden screen forming a balustrade consists of two parts: the lower part or base of solid wood and the upper part of pierced wood. The lower part has a height of 0.3–0.5 meters, while the upper pierced part has a height of 0.6–0.8 meters, so the total height of the balustrade varies between 1.1 and 1.3 meters. The pierced area of the balustrade consists of longitudinal wooden boards up to 0.10–0.12 meters in width; in large ornamental units, these may reach a width of 0.20 meters. The boards have an average thickness of 1 cm. Each board contains a complete ornamental unit in the centers of the lower and upper parts, which are carved with a chisel. The board also contains a half-ornamental unit at either side of the lower and upper parts, which are formed by wood sawing. The balustrade is assembled by fixing the boards beside each other and tucking their upper and lower ends into the balustrade's rail. The pierced part of the balustrade is usually made of good-quality, durable wood, such as athil, sycamore, or beach wood.

The pierced wooden part of the balustrade may be one whole panel (plate 35a), or it may be divided into panels of three equal sizes (plate 38b). In some examples the balustrade consists of one square panel in the middle surrounded by two rectangular panels at either side (plates 41b and 45). Sometimes, the balustrade is divided into five square panels of different ornamental units, which are repeated in another story of the same building (plate 42b). The solid wooden part of the balustrade is formed mainly of wooden sheet panels.

Wooden Screen Ornamentation
Lower-part Ornamentation

There are two types of ornamentation found in the bases of the balustrade: plant and geometric. The plant decorations include stems, twigs, and leaves in modified Rumi arabesque—the kind of ornamentation that could be seen in Rumi architecture during the last quarter of the nineteenth century. In Upper (Southern) Egyptian houses these shapes have been used in moderation. They have been pre-fabricated in special workshops and assembled with the use of adhesives and nails (plates 41b and 42b).

The local geometric ornamentation is far more common; it consists of rectangular, rhomboid (plate 43), and square figures (plates 53 and 54a). There are two kinds of rectangular figures: short and long. The short rectangle characteristically looks like a cartouche, is found inside a cavity, and is distinguished by its circular ends. It also contains engraved ornaments. These rectangles are placed in a special order, with a pair placed in a horizontal position followed by another in a vertical position (figure 3).

The large rectangles are distinguished by projected rhomboid shapes inside them with two protruding bosses in the middle (plate 43). These large rectangles are then followed by squares or circles containing protruding bosses (figure 4). In some examples, projected rhombuses in different sizes decorate the lower part of the balconies (plates 33 and 34b), and doors (plate 36).

Figure 3

Figure 4

Upper-part Ornamentation

The upper part of the wooden screen of a gallery balcony consists of the pierced wood of various ornamental units. One of the most common units in these screens has an arabesque pattern.

The word 'arabesque' refers to a form of artistic decoration in which ornamental units, such as plant leaves, stems, branches, and so on are interlocked, intertwined, and branched in such a way as to inspire one's imagination and contemplation.

Arabesque ornaments are linked to the emergence of the Samarra style, also known as Arabesque, named after Samara City, which was founded in AH 221/835 CE.[17] The emergence of the arabesque style heralded the most characteristic feature of Islamic art to have developed after two centuries of influence by Byzantine and Sassanid art. In addition to plants and geometric elements, this style was also distinguished by Arabic letters, their characters significantly modified by abstraction. This style had been greatly developed over time, and today reflects the special features of the region in which it has taken root. Arabesque is one of those ornamental arts that reflects the core of the Islamic faith; in principle, Islamic art avoids figurative representation or the ascribing of realistic ratios to the dimensions of human and animal bodies.

During the first three decades of the twentieth century, Upper Egyptian towns witnessed the revival of pierced-wood screens in balustrades of various types of balconies. The use of pierced wood as a method of screening and decoration is an old tradition dating back to the Fatimid period. One prominent example is the wooden portable niche of Sayyida Ruqayya, AH sixth century/twelfth century CE (now in the Museum of Islamic Art in Cairo). Besides the frieze inscribed with Kufic script and the geometric ornamentation that decorate the upper part of the niche, there is a transverse panel of pierced wood 1.35 x 0.22 meters in size. The panel consists of seven wide pieces of 0.18 x 0.12 meters, and six narrow pieces of 0.18 x 0.08 meters. Both types of pieces feature the same motifs, but to larger or smaller scale (figure 5).

Figure 5

Figure 6

Figure 7

Another old example of screening using pierced wood can be seen in the lintel of the wooden door of the tomb of al-Sultan al-Mansur Qalawun, which was built in AH 683–84/1284–85 CE, and also in the wooden screens that surround the cenotaph. The lintel consists of wooden boards of upper and lower solid portions, each one fifth the height of the board, while the middle portion with a height three-fifths of that of the board is characteristically made of pierced wood (figure 6). The upper part of the wooden screen of the cenotaph consists of longitudinal panels, each having between five and seven wooden boards of 0.18–0.25 meters' width (figure 7).

Upper Egyptian Arabesque

The revival of the practice of using pierced wood for the purpose of screening residential buildings in towns in Upper Egypt took on new artistic forms as craftsmen and artists in Upper Egypt developed and created their own type of arabesque, which drew on special motifs. The techniques used to make the pierced wood were part of a much older tradition, however. Some of these new motifs are widespread; for example, the geometric type of arabesque (B37) that decorates the balustrades of the gallery balcony of a house in Dayrut al-Sharif (Asyut Governorate) is the same type of arabesque as that seen on the balustrade of the reporter's tribune *(dikkat al-muballigh)* in the Mosque of al-Sit Numila[18] in Minya, some three hundred kilometers north, and which was built in AH 1317/1899 CE. Other motifs or units are restricted to a particular town. One such motif, which is found in Mallawi (Minya Governorate), is the arabesque of plant-shaped units. This type of arabesque is executed by perforation of a shape similar to the Arabic letter و *(waw)* in the wooden board. This letter consists of a rounded upper part connected with a curved or arched lower part. By assembling these perforated wooden boards on the balustrade, the various shapes and sizes of plant-leaf units emerge to form this special type of arabesque.

Pierced shapes are usually designed in pairs, with the two shapes that constitute a pair facing either in opposite directions or in the same way. In the first case the convexity or concavity of the two shapes may be facing (figure 8). In the second case the two shapes may be directed to the left or the right (figure 9). Usually, each board of wood contains between two and four pairs of these perforated shapes, which may appear in an upright or inverted position (figure 10). The upright pairs of these shapes enclose inverted shapes of plant-leaf units (figure 8), unlike the inverted pairs, which enclose straight shapes of plant leaf units (figure 10).

The characteristic shapes, and also the sizes, of the plant-leaf units are greatly influenced by three things: first, the shape and size of the perforated contour; second, the distance between the two shapes; third, whether or not the curved parts of each pair of shapes are joined or separated from each other.

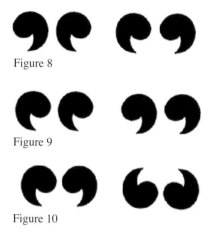

Figure 8

Figure 9

Figure 10

When the pierced *waw*-shapes are thick, short, and separate from each other, various shapes and sizes of the wider part of a plant leaf can be discerned between them (B1 and B2). If each of the two pierced *waw*-shapes has a thin curve and they are wide apart, the resulting shape between them will be the same, but larger in size (B11). Sometimes, the shapes have a long arch. In this case, if the distance between the two shapes is wide, the result will be a semi-complete plant-leaf unit (B8), but if the distance between the two shapes is narrow, a complete trefoiled leaf can be observed (B9). In other cases the و shape motifs were arranged with other motifs, such as arrow-heads and **V** shape motifs, in such a manner as to result in quintuple leaves (B13). It is interesting to note that the lower part of the wide part of pierced wood of the portable niche of al-Sayyida Ruqayya consists of و shape motifs (figure 5) that enclose the shape of a wider half of a plant leaf. When the two arches of the و shapes are large, long, and joined to each other, the result is an arrow-headed plant leaf unit (B19).

To understand the aesthetic as well as the artistic aspects of Upper Egyptian arabesque, one has to realize the connection between three relationships. The first is the relationship between solid and void. As in the previous type of arabesque, the void resulting from the و shapes (negative areas) creates the plant-leaf units (positive areas). So there is a mutual relationship between solid and void, which at the same time reflects the relationship between light (void) and shadow (solid).

The second relationship is that of the connections between the shapes of ornamental units, be they one or several units together, and the shapes of the other units that are spread onto the entire screen. In plate 34a and B36 we notice in the screen a large circular or oval unit; this unit interlocks with another, small unit that consists of a rectangle with six projections. This rectangle contains within it another shape, smaller in size and consisting of two trefoiled leaves that are joined together and point in opposite directions. One's eye moves continually between these different-sized shapes, from the large to the small, and from the small to the large, giving a sense of transition from partial to whole; that is, from the small units of ornaments to the ornamentation as a whole, which spreads out and extends over the entire screen.

The third relationship that helps us to understand and interpret the arabesque is the distance between onlooker and balustrade. This distance greatly affects the perceived shape of the ornamental units. The balustrade may be found in the first, second, or third story of the building and the shapes of the ornamental units change accordingly. For example in plate 46b and B43 one notices in the lower part of each board two small voids in the shape of irregular figures that are separate from each other. These two figures look joined and take the shape of an arch, however, when they are in the upper part of the board. Hence the shape of the same unit may change depending on the onlooker's distance from the unit, and consequently his or her angle of vision.

One may therefore conclude that one of the arabesque's characteristics is its ability to continually generate and form new ornamental units out of essentially small numbers of existing ornamental units. These new units emerge as a result of a realization on the part of the onlooker of void–mass and light–shadow relationships or of the unit as a whole according to one's distance from the shapes. The arrangement of the shapes fulfills the objective of creating a transition in the mind's eye from physical place relations on a plane (the ornamental units) to an abstract impression.

The place relation is an essentially sensuous and concrete one and is characterized by finiteness, whereas the extensive relation is a cognitive relation and is characterized by infinity. Thus the aim or objective of arabesque ornamentation is contemplation, that is, the transition from partial relation to universal relation, which is characterized by abstraction.

This transition from place relation to extensive relation, from finiteness to the infinite, from the perceptible to the imperceptible, can clearly be seen in Figure 11. The shape resulting from the void of two separate thick arches of ‫و‬ shaped letters, connected with the void of a **V** shape in the middle of the upper and lower part of the wooden board, give quintuple leaves (whether in a straight or inverted position). Also, the shape resulting from the void of two separate, moderately wide ‫و‬ shaped letters, connected with the void of an elongated arrow head in the peripheries of the upper and lower part of the wooden board, yields quintuple leaves of different shapes (whether in straight or inverted position). The two

Figure 11 (B13)

shapes of the leaves are found within the rectangular shape of the wooden board. Intersecting with this rectangle is an imagined oval shape, formed, through the contemplation of the onlooker, in two steps; the first step occurs when the onlooker observes the two arms of the arrowhead shape in the peripheries between the boards, which causes his/her sight to be directed either right or left. The two ends of the imagined shape are completed in the second step, when the onlooker's sight is directed to the void of the **V** shape present in the middle of the upper or lower part of the board. The onlooker makes a connection between each of the imaginary joined oval shapes, to simultaneously realize another big oval shape.

The imagined oval shape that the onlooker can deduce in this arabesque is not originally found in the board: only the quintuple leaf-shapes are noticeable and perceptible. In this example of arabesque, the transition from real and perceptible to imaginary oval shapes is achieved through a mental abstraction that reflects the concept of extension, which is essentially a mental process that finally reveals the objective and significance of the arabesque.

Another, closely related type of arabesque is found in Mallawi (Minya Governorate). It depends on triangular shapes positioned in rows, each one opposing the other. The arms of the triangular **V** shapes may or may not have rounded ends (plate 38b, B18, B23), and may be of thin (plate 36a, B20) or thick (plate 43, B19) width. The arrangement of these shapes calls forth arrow-headed motifs or units, either in straight or inverted positions, and these motifs create a variety of other shapes in between.

As well as the group of arabesque styles based on و shaped units, and the group based on **V**-shaped units, there are the geometric-shape group (plates 43 and 44b), the manifold-shape group. In this last group, there is a cross-shaped motif in the center and at the peripheries of each wooden board. Besides this motif, there are two separate but facing curved irregular shapes in the upper and lower parts. These two motifs look like an arch when seen from a distance (plate 46b), and create and develop manifold figures in between (B42 and B43).

Some balustrades of gallery balconies are divided into square panels. Each square has a special kind of ornamentation; one type is an arabesque of plant leaves, while the other panels have a geometric kind of arabesque, which may take the form of small four-sided units in different shapes and sizes formed by the intersection of large squares and circles (plate 42b, B32, B34, and B41). In some cases the square panels have a lattice orna-mentation going in different directions (plate 43, B48).

Besides the balustrades in the arabesque style there are other ornamenta-tions that are concentrated on a repetition of motifs and their units. Although their appearance depends upon the contrast between void and mass or light and shadow, they differ from the arabesque units in that they are devoid of interlocking and an intricacy between shapes, and they do not depend on the generation and emergence of shapes from other shapes. We can distinguish three groups of these kinds of ornamentations.

1. Longitudinal-opening ornamentations: these consist of longitudinal slits that differ in length and width, giving long, short, thin, and broad open-ings. They also differ in their manner of arrangement. It can be noted in plate 50b and B54 that the upper part of the screen has a broad frieze in the center comprising longitudinal slits of differing length; one finds a long one followed by a short one. These slits are arranged in a circle. Below and above this frieze is another type of frieze consisting of thin

and short slits along the screen. There is a second kind of slit pattern, where the slits differ in width and length and are arranged in such a way that a wide and short slit is followed by a thin and long one, the wide slit having a rhombus shape at either end (plate 50b, B56). Then there is a third type of slit decoration, that found in Qena, which takes the shape of two center friezes of wide and thin slits; in the upper and lower part of each wooden board there are two rows of triangular shapes, each facing the other (plate 51, B57).

2. Fret-shaped ornamentations:[19] this group is characterized by oval shapes that interlock with each other to give the impression of netting. Intersected with these oval units, which are arranged vertically, is a strip of twists, which extends horizontally across (plate 49, B47).

3. Interlaced-shaped ornamentations: these are characterized by the repetition of different shapes and sizes of motifs, which include pyriform (plate 58, B62), bell (plate 60, B61), triangular, and oval shapes (plate 61, B31).

Screening of Usual Balconies

The rule "neither mischief nor reciprocal harm" has been strictly followed in the screening of the usual balcony formations of the medium- and small-scale houses of Upper Egyptian towns, in order to maintain privacy for the members of the household. By applying this rule, these balconies have been characterized by a number of properties. First, this type of balcony is totally enclosed on three sides by wooden screens (thus differing from the balconies of the Neoclassical architectural style of wrought-iron balustrades, also seen in the towns of upper Egypt). Second, the wooden screens are 1.6–1.7 meters high, that is, they are raised to the height of a man (plates 53, 54, 55a, and 57b). This rule has a few exceptions, as for instance in Mallawi (Minya Governorate), where another type of balcony, one with low balusters, can be found, with its height varying between 1.1 and 1.2 meters. Thirdly, because these balconies contain high wooden screens, they have small windows in various shapes in the screens' upper part in order to allow members of the household to see out (plates 53, 54a, and 57b).

The system of balcony screening consists of a base of solid wood with a pierced-wood area above it. The base varies between one-third and half the height of the balcony. In some examples, the whole screen is made of pierced wood, as we can see in Beni Suef (plate 60). In other cases, the total height of the balconies is made of solid wood, as can be found in apartment buildings (plate 56).

The base of the usual balcony in Tima comprises large squares or rhombuses in different sizes (plates 53 and 54a; C10 and C11). In Girga the balcony's base is characteristically decorated by projected rhombuses in different sizes (plate 33).

The upper part of the balcony screen, which usually takes the form of pierced wood, may be divided into equal square panels of different types of arabesque (plate 38b) as in Tahta. In some examples the whole part is screened by differently shaped panels of lattice wood as seen in Nag' Hammadi (plate 55a). In Beni Suef and Asyut balcony balustrades are screened with many types of pierced wood (plates 58, 59, and 60).

The Shape and Decoration of the Upper Egyptian House's Roofline

Due to the smallness of housing plots in Upper Egyptian towns, the top story of upper- and middle-class houses, as well as that of low-income houses, played a very important role in household activities. Since the first and second stories were used as living quarters, the house's top story was used for household work, such as cooking, preparing livestock, washing dishes and clothes, and poultry breeding.

To avoid any "detriment of unveiling," especially for members of the family who could be found on the roof of a house, rules of *fiqh* also regulated the heights of the side walls of roofs between adjacent houses, as well as the heights of walls that overlooked the road. Inasmuch as one neighbor must not unveil the other, one can still observe the application of this tradition in some of the houses built in the town of Rashid (northern Egypt), which were built during the Ottoman period: "screens of bricks 1.75 meters in height have been erected to separate two adjacent roofs with the owners' aim of using this roof freely for any family activities, therefore avoiding the detriment of unveiling and offering privacy, like the screen that separates the two roofs of the Galal and al-Mizzuni houses."[20]

The houses of towns in Upper Egypt (whether in the Nile Valley or the Western Desert) still reflect the tradition of erecting high brick walls between neighboring houses, as seen in the houses in Rashid. In al-Qasr the roofs are surrounded by high walls reaching up to one to two meters in height, known as *al-satir* (the curtain), to protect the privacy of the inhabitants.[21] These walls are traditionally constructed in the form of longitudinal openings in al-Qasr (plate 75). Besides the brick screen between two adjacent houses, there is also a wooden screen that has the same function, especially when parts of one of the houses project too closely to a neighboring house. An example of the wooden screen can be seen between two adjacent houses in Bir Abu Shamiya Street in Minya. Residence no. 56 has a projected bay that is about a meter away from its neighbor, which consequently has a two-meter-high wooden screen on its roof (plate 63).

The principle of avoiding any "detriment of unveiling" and maintaining one's privacy also plays an important role in regulating the height of the wall on a roof that looks upon the façade of an adjacent house. This wall serves not only a practical purpose, but an aesthetic one as well, as it is used to beautify the front view of the house. Upper Egyptian towns exhibit different styles of pediment and roofline. One of these is the Eclectic style, which was greatly influenced by European styles (plates 34a and 49). But in many examples local styles prevail. This consists of a pediment with or without two piers in each corner of the building. The shape of the pediment may be trefoil (plate 27), curved (plate 68), stepped (plate 66), or pyramidal (plate 51). Usually there is a hole in the upper part of the pediment. The pier may have a blunt end (plate 32) or a pyramidal end that looks like an obelisk (plate 65). Sometimes the edge of the pediment is demarcated by a very simple projected cornice. In some examples the pediment has stucco decorations and is topped by an eagle with outstretched wings (plate 65).

The Influence of *Fiqh* and the Emergence of Two Doorways in the Houses of Upper Egypt

The rules of *fiqh* and their judgment to avoid any "detriment of unveiling" had a great impact on the location of doorways in Upper Egyptian houses as well as on their structure and character.

In this respect, doorways were usually positioned in such a way as not to face each other. Some of the most striking examples remaining in Cairo from the Ottoman period bear witness to this. They are the two doorways of Bayt al-Kiritliya (AH 1041/1631 CE) and the Amna bint Salim house (AH 947/1540 CE). Both doors are located in a narrow road opposite each other: "While the doorway of Bayt al-Kiritliya is placed at its southwest side, the door of the house of Amna bint Salim opposite is placed at the end of its north side. Hence the doors do not face each other."[22] This tradition can still be observed in the houses of al-Qasr town in Dakhla Oasis.

Regarding the structure and character of the doorways, the architecture of Cairene upper-class houses in the Ottoman period was characterized by a bent doorway. It was designed in such a way that the external doorway would not be aligned with the door leading to the house's courtyard or its interior. This 'divided' doorway consisted of two parts—the outside door and, directly behind it, a square or rectangular area known as the *durqa'a*. The *durqa'a* had a side opening that led, via a corridor, to the courtyard. So the *durqa'a* and the corridor together made up this curved passage and fully satisfied the required purpose of not aligning external and internal doorways. These types of double doorways, constructed in the Ottoman period, were considered a continuation of the traditions of dwelling architecture, particularly in the palaces that had been built since the Bahri Mamluk period, such as the palace of Aaliyn Aq, AH 693/1293 CE. The palace's doorway on its north side had a door leading to a *durqa'a* measuring 4.5 meters square.[23] On the east side of the *durqa'a*, there was an opening leading to the palace's interior courtyard.

In the nineteenth century, a change took place in the upper-class houses that had been built in accordance with the Rumi style, where the 'bent-doorway' system disappeared, to be replaced by another system where the doorways opened up into a 'passageway' leading directly to the house's courtyard. However, in order to follow legal rules, the doorway as well as the passageway did not lead directly to the house's courtyard, but to the side of the building at its far end, and in such a manner that the courtyard area was shielded from the larger part of the street. The second change in the new system, which venerated privacy, was the name and structure of the reception unit. The new reception unit, which was known as the *salamlik*, replaced the old Ottoman reception unit, the *takhtabush*. The *takhtabush* is located on the ground floor, which opens onto the courtyard facing north; it is higher than the courtyard level by one step, or 0.30 meters. The *takhtabush*, which does not project from but is at the same level as the wall, is usually supported by one column in its center.[24] The word *salamlik* (from *al-salam 'alik*) means the place where male guests gathered, as opposed to *haramlik* (from *haram 'alik*, 'it's forbidden for you'), which is where the female guests gathered together. Unlike the *takhtabush*, the *salamlik* projects from the wall by 1.5 to 2.0 meters, is elevated above the courtyard level by three to four steps, and has a pediment resting on two wooden columns. The steps lead to a platform followed by a two-leaf door that opens into a big hall bordered by two to four rooms.[25]

Despite the limited number of towns in the southern part of the Nile Valley that have been influenced by the Rumi style, a small number of the houses in these towns featured a good imitation of this style, especially of the *salamlik* block. The limited area of these towns, enclosed within the narrow belt of the valley's agricultural areas and between the eastern and western mountains, made it difficult to find the interior space necessary for the courtyard and *salamlik* block. Instead, the *salamlik* block had been placed in one of the façades of the house, which faced north, and opened onto an outer courtyard (plate 16). So these houses had two separate entrances, a private one for family members and their relatives, and another for guests. In the case of poorer dwellings and houses situated in the town's trading district, it was hard to find an outer courtyard that had enough room for a reception unit. This situation led its inhabitants to make use of other available space within a house. Some parts of the ground floor only could be earmarked for such a reception unit. In this instance, the two-doorway system was not used.

While upper-class houses retained the historic name of the reception unit, *salamlik*, the reception unit in middle- and low-income houses was referred to as the *mandara*, but was popularly known as the *madyafa*,[26] the place where visitors and guests of the family came together. The *mandara* had several functions, and was used for festivals, funeral ceremonies, recitals of the Qur'an during Ramadan nights, and receiving people's congratulations during feasts and on other occasions, such as weddings.

The two-doorway system can still be found in upper- and middle-class houses in the small and large towns of Upper Egypt, for instance in Sohag, where, in the southern district, one can find a large house that belongs to the Fahmy family. The door leading to the reception unit that opens onto the outdoor courtyard is located in al-Corniche Street, which is the main street, whereas the main door is located in Hammam Street, which is a narrow side street (plate 35a). The same goes for the house built on the corner of al-Corniche and al-Qaffas streets; the door leading directly to the reception unit is in al-Corniche Street, while the other door, the main one (plate 37), is in the side street, al-Qaffas Street. In Qena, we can see more of these types of double doorways; in the house built on the corner of Grand Mosque Street and Abdallah Street, the main doorway looks out into Abdallah Street. Another door, leading to a small courtyard in front of the reception unit, is on Grand Mosque Street (plate 1a). In Minya, the house on 41 Sidi Habib Street has the main doorway followed by another doorway leading to the exterior courtyard of the house, which has a place allocated for a reception unit facing north; that is, the two doorways lie on the same street. One of them is wide and heavily decorated—this is the main doorway (plate 14c)—while the other is small with minute decorations. The house located on the corner of al-Madrasa al-Amiriya and Sidi Habib streets also has two doorways. The main one is on 15 Sidi Habib Street, while on the other side of the house, facing north, there is a small door leading to the mandara unit, which looks onto the house's exterior courtyard. This part of the building borders al-Madrasa al-Amiriya Street, a branch of Muhammad Badawi Street (plate 17).

The Shape and Decoration of Upper Egyptian Doorways

The doorways of houses built in Upper Egyptian towns between the late nineteenth and first half of the twentieth century can be classified into three categories. The first category includes those doorways that are related to the Rumi style. This style of doorway is usually found in large-scale buildings and opulent houses. The second category includes the doorways that reflect a combination of the general features of European-style doorways with their usual five divisions (which, from top to bottom, are: plate-band area, upper section, cornice, lower section, and threshold), and the usual stucco or stone ornamentation of the Rumi-style entrance. This style of doorway can be seen in wealthy twentieth-century family houses. The third category of doorway is a mixed form, which combines some features from the two previous categories with local elements, such as iron motifs on a fanlight and a wooden frame around a door. This style of doorway can be found in a wide variety of small-scale, low-income houses as well as twentieth century neo-Islamic-style houses, particularly in small towns.

Rumi-style Doorways

Large towns in the south of Egypt have many houses that were built in the Rumi style. One of these examples is the house located in al-Sayyida Hurriya Street in Beni Suef, which was built in AH 1304/1886 CE, as indicated in the hub of the fanlight (plate 69b). It is a two-story, plain-façade building with elongated vertical lattice windows.

The fanlight of its Rumi-style doorway consists of a number of spokes that protrude from a hub.[27] Enclosed in between these spokes is a variety of decorative motifs, which include circles, semicircles, or pear-shaped motifs with rounded ends. The last motif is the most common plant decoration unit of these fanlights houses, even in Upper Egyptian towns. The oldest pear-shaped motif dates back to the brass three-windowed public fountain (figure 12) annexed to the mosque of Sulayman Agha al-Silahdar in al-Mu'izz Street, AH 1225/1839 CE. These motifs are made in such a manner that the broad and pointed ends alternate with each other.

Figure 12

The iron spokes that protrude from the hub of the fanlight are fixed to the motifs by two methods: with molten lead, making different shapes (E26 and E28), or by heating small iron strips (known as clamps) to high temperatures. The iron strips are wrapped around the parts and firmly knocked on. When the temperature cools, the parts become fixed firmly together (E17–E22).

The two doorways situated in Hammam (plate 35b) and Bashmuhandis streets (plate 70) off al-Corniche Street in Sohag also date back to the last quarter of the nineteenth century. Both houses' doorways reflect Rumi-style traditional architecture and decorations.

The forms, partitions, and decorations of the Rumi-style doorways of Upper Egyptian houses gradually became intermingled with the early-twentieth-century European-doorways style. There are remaining examples of such doorways that combine the two styles; for instance, the doorway of the house on 41 Sidi Habib Street in Minya (plate 14c). Here the nineteenth-century Rumi style is clearly identifiable by its parts and decorations, and by the division of the doorway into an arch area containing fanlight, entablature area, spandrel, jamb, and pilaster. Plants and geometric decorations can be seen in the pilaster and jamb area, and garland decorations or arabesque in the spandrel area. However, it is also notable that the doorway has a two-leaf door, with the upper panel leaf in wrought iron.

Local-style Doorways

A special style of doorways in Upper Egyptian towns materialized in the early period of the twentieth century. These doorways were distinguished by certain characteristics. First, the divisions and decorations inspired by the Rumi-style doorways were ignored. Second, the divisions and decorations of the twentieth-century European-style doors were also ignored; in other words, the wrought iron of the upper panel was absent in this style of door. Third, the door was surrounded by a broad wooden frame, either on both sides (jamb area), or on the upper part of the door, its width varying between 0.12 and 0.15 meters, and possibly reaching up to 0.20 meters. Fourth was the appearance of unique motifs in wrought iron on the fanlights, either in semicircular or in rectangular form.

Doorways with these four characteristics represented the local style. The doors in this style appeared to lack the usual five divisions. The door leaf consisted of one panel decorated by means of projecting wooden strips in the shape of a semicircular arch at the top of the leaf. Some examples of these doors still keep to the tradition of having a threshold area (plate 72).

In the case of doorways with fanlights, these were also enclosed by wooden frames of dentiform decorations (plate 72). In a house's doorway in Tima, it was noted that this wooden frame, which surrounded the sides of the door, extended to take in the fanlight area. So this frame looked like a big wooden rectangle encompassing the fanlight and the door (plates 54b and 73). It was also noted that the frame at the sides of the door was somewhat broader than its usual width, reaching 0.20 meters (plate 54b). Wooden pediments projected above some of these doors (plate 54b).

Some of the characteristic features of these doorways in the local style are the special motifs on the wrought-iron fanlights. The semicircular fanlights are characterized by units with motifs in the form of iron scrolls which are found in various folds next to pear-shaped motifs in different sizes. These features are quite complicated (plate 71). The rectangular fanlight of these doorways also contains units in the shape of beautiful rhombuses (E35). These doorways and doors are also often distinguished by their various colors. They are made of burned bricks, covered with a layer of mortar, then plastered with lime, after which a color is finally added. Lime plastering has been used in Egypt since the pharaonic age, and there is much evidence of this, for example, "a wall belonging to the ancient state painted by lime plastering, or one finds in Tell al-Amarna many interior walls covered with plastering."[28] As for the doors, they are covered with a layer of linen oil mixed with colors. Sandpaper is used to smooth the wood, which is then covered with a layer of ceruse (lead sulfate, which is a mix of white lead and boiled linen oil), and lastly the door is painted with a mixture of boiled linen oil and zinc powder (lead oxide) mixed with oil-based colors. "This method has been used in making ornamental units since the Ottoman period."[29]

In the third decade of the twentieth century, double-leaf doors appeared that were made entirely of iron. Their lower part, which was one-third of the door's height, was solid, but the upper part, constituting two-thirds of the door's height, consisted of lengths of iron in the form of serpent tails arranged in a zigzag shape. Crisscrossing the longitudinal units was a unit that took the shape of a big crescent. There was a triangular area of different ornamental motifs shaped as crescents on top of the two leaves (plate 65).

The Structure and Decoration of the Doorways of al-Qasr Oasis Houses

Many large- and middle-sized families of landowners and merchants live in the city of al-Qasr in the New Valley governorate, in the Western Desert, eight kilometers from Dakhla. Most of their houses date back to the seventeenth century. These houses have been well-maintained to this day, as descendants of the old families have lived in the same houses for many generations, the result of a strong extended-family culture.

The phenomenon of the two-doorway system can clearly be observed in al-Qasr. The first doorway, which is the main one, usually overlooks the main road, while the second, the family doorway, is usually smaller in size and situated on the side narrow lane. The main doorways have two characteristics: First is the local-style type of decoration and second is the wooden lintel on which is engraved information about family ancestors as well as the builder's name.

The position and distribution of the two types of doorways is greatly influenced by the jurisprudential rule on avoiding any "detriment of unveiling." Hence, no one doorway faces directly onto any other doorway. It has been noted that 90 percent of the doorways in al-Qasr do not face each other.[30]

The main doorways are, moreover, set back from the façade wall by 0.30 to 0.40 meters. These doorways are decorated using two methods, depending on the type of bricks used; in the first method mud bricks are used to give form to the decorations. As seen in plate 78, the doorway

Figure 13: *Ma'qali*

is decorated with three courses of bricks. The first course is perpendicular to the doorway arch, followed by another course of two rows of bricks set at angles to each other. This course is surrounded by a third row and consists of one course of bricks. Bricks are also used to form oblique *ma'qali* decorations in the area above the door arch, or simple *ma'qali* above the door lintel. The second method of decorating doorways depends on the use of *mangur* bricks as shown in plate 80. In this case, stepped-shape decorations are used, consisting of three bricks: two horizontal and one perpendicular in the middle. These shapes are arranged opposite each other, and are fixed by a layer of white gypsum (calcium sulfate).

The most important part that characterizes al-Qasr doorways is the wooden lintels. They consist of longitudinal blocks of a hard kind of timber known as athil wood, as it is mentioned in one of the ancient documents.[31] The surface of a block consists of various parts, including a large middle part that occupies four-fifths of the area. This part contains engraved inscriptions in Naskh script; these are either in one line, in larger print (plate 78b), or two lines, one beneath the other, in smaller print. In this case one will find a separation between the lines (plate 79b). The first lines of these inscriptions start with the *basmala* ("In the name of God, the Merciful, the Compassionate"); then the Qur'anic verse, *Udkhuluha bi-salamin aminin* ("Enter in peace and security"; Qur'an 15:46), followed by a partial verse *wa zayyannaha li-l-nazirin* ("we adorned it for the spectators"; Qur'an

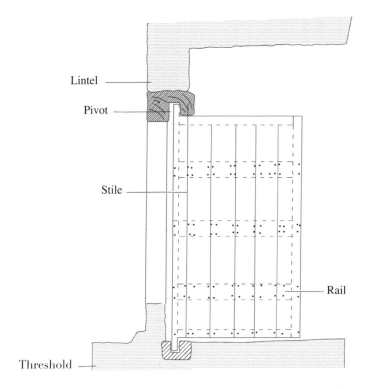

Figure 14: Design of one-leaf doors of the nineteenth century (after an illustration in *Mari Girgis, Village de Haute-Egypte* (1988), p. 45, by Nessim-Henry Henein)

15:16). These lines also include the names of the head of the household, his father, and his grandfather. Usually, the construction date of the house is added (as is shown in plate 77), going back to AH 1082/1671 CE. The name of the man who constructed the lintel is written in very small letters below the first or second sentence. Sometimes the name of the builder is written in two horizontal lines on the farthest left side of the lintel, separated from the rest of the inscription, as shown in plate 77 (here the master is 'Abd al-Mu'izz al-Naggar). The edges of the inscriptions are usually made up of twisted decorations. The second part of the lintel comprises the decoration area, which takes up the two ends of the plate.

These decorated parts are separated from the inscription area by vertically twisted lines and usually comprise two large circular bosses, one at either side of the inscription, or two small bosses, one above the other, also at either side. Be it one boss or two, they all have small geometric figures engraved on them, such as triangles (plates 77 and 78b), parallelograms, or whirlpools (plate 79b). The doorways of the al-Qasr houses are all single-leaf doors that consist of longitudinal plates that are fixed next to each other on wooden rails nailed to the doors. These doors are made of jujube wood, which is very hard and which has been aged over a long period of time. A door moves by means of two projections, one each at the top and bottom of the hinge stile, fixed in two grooves in the doorway's lintel and threshold.

The Older-style Doorways in Upper Egyptian Towns

The farthest towns of the Nile Valley, like Qus (Qena governorate) and Qena, still have these styles of doorways, which are older than the Rumi-style doorways, and resemble al-Qasr doorways.

The shape of the inscription area and the number of circular bosses in the lintel differ from those in the al-Qasr lintels. The inscription areas are engraved inside twelve rectangles or cartouches, placed directly above the other. These cartouches are arranged in three groups, two in the jamb area and one in the door area. Each group of cartouches is surrounded by a twisted frame, and the cartouche has either rounded or pointed ends. The phrases inside these cartouches read either vertically or horizontally. In this type of lintel there are five bosses with different motif shapes (F5, F6).

In the lintel shown in plate 80 there are twelve cartouches with rounded ends allotted for the inscriptions. They are arranged in three groups, which are separated by five bosses. The inscription area starts on the farthest right-hand side of the doorjamb. The text of the first two cartouches is displayed vertically and says: "This is by the grace," and the lower one, "of my Lord." The other two cartouches are also displayed vertically and read "The head of wisdom" in the upper cartouche and "the fear of the Lord" in the lower cartouche. Directly above the door there are four cartouches which read horizontally and say: "Glory for the Lord, in the heavens, peace be upon the land, and delight for the people." On the left side of the lintel there are four cartouches, separated by a boss into pairs. These cartouches contain inscriptions that are displayed vertically. The first two cartouches say that this house was renovated; the second two say that the date of this renovation was in "Bermhat 1598."[32] It can also be noted that the circular bosses that separate the inscription areas contain many triangular, quadruple, hexagonal, and octagonal motifs. This method of dividing a door lintel into various inscription areas separated by circular bosses can also be seen in the door lintel of no. 2 Darb al-'Umari in Quws. In the remaining part of this lintel, there are five inscription areas separated by four bosses (plate 81). The inscription areas take the shape of two cartouches, one on top of the other, either large or small with pointed ends. These cartouches are enclosed within a frame of twisted ornaments. The first area on the doorjamb to the right contains the phrase "In the name of God, the Beneficent, the Merciful," followed by an area of circular decorations. Then there is another area that reads "*Inna fatahna laka fathan mubinan*" ("We have granted you a manifest victory"; Qur'an 48:1). It should be noted here that the ornamental circular bosses contain star figures with six and eight heads.

Plate 82 shows a Qena doorway dating back to the late nineteenth century that is very similar to the doorway styles of the mosques and caravanserais that were built in Upper Egyptian towns during the eighteenth century. These doorways are in the shape of a trefoiled arch and entirely decorated with *mangur* bricks.

The *mangur* decorations in this doorway are richer and more precise than those found on, for example, the doorway of the al-Qurashi family house in al-Qasr (plate 78). These richer decorations have a star-plate and, in addition, hexagonal and square figures.

Conclusion

Two architectural trends were introduced into Egypt during the nineteenth century: the Rumi style during the period of Muhammad 'Ali (1805–49), and the European styles during the period of the Khedive Ismail (1863–79).

The European architectural styles that were widespread during the 1863–1914 period were the Neoclassical, Neo-Baroque, Art Nouveau, Mediterranean, Eclectic, and neo-Islamic styles. These two trends were subsequently imitated by native architects in the towns of Upper Egypt.

Besides the imitation of these two trends, Upper Egyptian towns developed and created their own eclectic or local architectural style. One cultural factor, deriving from Islamic jurisprudence, which had a great impact on the three elements constituting building façades, is the rule that calls for the avoidance of the "detriment of unveiling." These three elements include (1) perforations such as mashrabiyas, windows, and balconies; (2) pediments and rooflines; and finally (3) the doorway block.

The balustrades of gallery balconies, as well as the parapets of the usual balconies, are screened by pierced-wood screens, some of which exhibit arabesque decoration. Interestingly, Upper Egyptian towns developed a unique type of arabesque composed of special motifs, which we can call 'Sa'idi,' or Upper Egyptian, arabesque.

Some of these motifs, which are executed by use of the ﻭ shape, are highly characteristic of towns like Mallawi or Girga. Other types of arabesque that draw on geometric motifs are widespread in various other towns.

Upper Egyptian towns exhibit different shapes of pediment and roofline. Some of these are in the Eclectic style, which is highly imitative of European styles, although the local style nevertheless prevailed. It consists of a pediment, with or without two piers, in each corner of the building. The pediment may be trefoiled, curved, stepped, or pyramidal in shape. The piers may have blunt or pyramidal ends. Sometimes, the pediment is surrounded by a simple projected cornice. In some cases, the pediment has a stucco decoration topped by a large eagle with outstretched wings.

Upper Egyptian towns have four categories of doorway. The first is related to the Rumi style, as we can see in Beni Suef, Minya, and Sohag. There are also doorways that exhibit a combination of the European style and the stucco decoration of the Rumi style. The third category includes the local-style doorways with rounded or rectangular shape fanlights. These fanlights display highly unique scroll or geometric motifs, as in Tahta. The fourth category relates to the old doorways of al-Qasr in Dakhla Oasis, with their characteristic engraved inscription wooden lintels dating back to the seventeenth century. This type of doorway can still be found in towns far south, such as Qus, Qena, and Tahta.

Notes

1 Muhammad A. Rashad, "Qasray Hayat al-Nufus wa Sayf al-Nasr bi madinat Mallawi, muhafazat al-Minya: dirasa athariya fanniya" (MSc in Archaeology, Faculty of Archaeology, Cairo University, 2007), 241.

2 Ali M. Qandil, "An Analysis of Architecture Styles in Cairo's Downtown, 1863–1914," MSc in Architecture, Faculty of Engineering, Cairo University, 2000, 270.

3 Qandil, "An Analysis of Architecture Styles," 118.

4 Tariq M. Saker, *Early Twentieth-century Islamic Architecture in Cairo* (Cairo: American University in Cairo Press, 1992), 76.

5 Qandil, "An Analysis of Architecture Styles," 285.

6 Qandil, "An Analysis of Architecture Styles," 286.

7 Qandil, "An Analysis of Architecture Styles," 285.

8 Qandil, "An Analysis of Architecture Styles," 143.

9 Qandil, "An Analysis of Architecture Styles," 285.

10 Ahmed M. Abdel-Gawad, *Enter in Peace: The Doorways of Cairo Homes 1872–1950* (Cairo: American University Press, 2007), 122.

11 Abdel-Gawad, *Enter in Peace*, 123.

12 Abdel-Gawad, *Enter in Peace*, 122–23.

13 Muhammad Amin and Layla Ibrahim, *al-Mustalahat al-mi'mariya fi-l-watha'iq al-mamlukiya* (Cairo: Qism al-Nashr bi-l-Jami'a al-Amirikiya bi-l-Qahira, 1990), 16.

14 Ibn al-Rami, *al-I'lam bi-ahkam al-bunyan* (Alexandria: Dar al-Ma'rifa al-Gami'iya, 1989), 54.

15 Ahmed G. Ahmed, "Athar al-bi'a 'ala al-'imara fi Misr ma' dirasa li-'imarat qura al-Sa'id" (Cairo: MSc in Architecture, Faculty of Fine Arts, Architecture Department, 1975), 69.

16 Qandil, "An Analysis of Architecture Styles," 303.

17 Su'ad Mahir, *al-Funun al-islamiya* (Cairo: Maktabat al-Usra, 2005), 322.

18 Gamal S. al-Bayyumi, "al-'Anasir al-mi'mariya wa-l-zukhrufiya bi masajid Misr al-wusta" (Cairo: MSc in Archaeology, Faculty of Archaeology, Cairo University, 2002), 202.

19 Gamal al-Tuni, *Atlas al-wihdat al-zukhrufiya* (Cairo: al-Katib al-Masri li-l-Tiba'a wa-l-Nashr, 1988), 2–14.

20 Khalid 'Izab, *Fiqh al-'imara al-islamiya* (Cairo: Dar al-Nashr li-l-Gami'at, 1997), 86.

21 Sa'd Shihab, *Baldat al-Qasr wa atharuha al-islamiya* (Cairo: Dar al-Afaq al-'Arabiya), 327.

22 'Izab, *Fiqh al-'imara*, 76.

23 Jacques Revault and Bernard Maury, *Palais et maisons du Caire du XIVe au XVIIIe siécle, 2* (Cairo: Institut français d'archéologie orientale du Caire, 1977), 20.

24 Rif'at Musa, *al-Wikalat wa-l-buyut al-islamiya fi Misr al-'uthmaniya* (Cairo: al-Dar al-Misriya al-Libnaniya, 1993), 225.

25 Madkur Pasha House, 13 al-Tabana street, al-Darb al-Ahmar district, and the house located on 3 Qasr al-Shawq, al-Gamaliya district in Cairo, are good examples of passageways that open onto an inner courtyard and of the structure and decoration of the *salamlik* block.

26 Muhammad 'Abd al-Hafiz, *al-Mustalahat al-mi'mariya fi watha'iq 'asr Muhammad 'Ali wa khulafa'uh, 1805–1879* (Cairo: n.p., 2005), 166.

27 Abdel-Gawad, *Enter in Peace*, 16.

28 B. Tiodarovitsh, *Mushkilat al-iskan fi-l-rif al-misri* (al-Munufiya: al-Markaz al-Dawli li-l-Tarbiya al-Asasiya, 1955), 140.

29 Shadya al-Disuqi, *al-Akhshab fi-l-'imara al-diniya bi-l-Qahira al-'uthmaniya* (Cairo: Maktabat Zahra' al-Sharq, 2003), 125.

30 Shihab, *Baldat al-Qasr*, 209.

31 Ibrahim 'Uthman, *al-Ashjar al-khashabiya* (Cairo: Matba'at al-I'timad, 1939), 145.

32 Bermhat is the fourth month of the Coptic calendar, equivalent to the period between 10 March and 8 April. The Coptic calendar year 1598 is equivalent to 1873 CE.

THE PLATES

Plate 1

B55

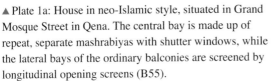

▲ Plate 1a: House in neo-Islamic style, situated in Grand Mosque Street in Qena. The central bay is made up of repeat, separate mashrabiyas with shutter windows, while the lateral bays of the ordinary balconies are screened by longitudinal opening screens (B55).

A2

◄Plate 1b: The lower and upper areas of the mashrabiya have rectangular panels with abstract motifs. The eaves are composed of longitudinal slit motifs (A2).

►Plate 1c: Local-style doorway surrounded by a decorated frame. The lintel has a rectangular wooden area decorated with abstract motifs (C1).

C1

Plate 2

A15

◀Plate 2a: Repeating separate-type mashrabiyas in each façade of a house in Qift (Qena Governorate). These mashrabiyas are very simple, with two-part shutter windows and a projected eave (A15).

▶ Plate 2b: Local-style doorway with a decorated wooden frame and a rectangular fanlight with pear-shaped motifs in wrought iron.

Plate 3

B50

◀Plate 3: Repeating separate-type mashrabiyas in each of the façades of a house in Mallawi (Minya Governorate) with projected eaves decorated above and below with plant motifs (A23). The whole body of each mashrabiya is covered with arabesque ornamentation (B50).

A23

Plate 4

◀Plate 4a: Repeating separate-type mashrabiyas of a house located in Bir Abu Shamiya Street in Minya. This mashrabiya is distinguished by its glass screening.

▼Plate 4b: Mashrabiya in three vertical parts. The middle part has windows of glass sheet panes. The upper part is composed of trefoil wooden tracery with projected eaves and upper and lower plant motifs (A22), and the base is made up of star-plate ornamentation (C2).

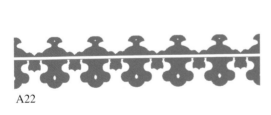

A22

C2

Plate 5

A16

◀ Plate 5a: A house in the neo-Islamic style in Grand Mosque Street in Qena with a traditionally shaped mashrabiya.

▶ Plate 5b: A mashrabiya with three shutter windows in its middle part. It is screened by three types of lathe-turned wood. Its upper part has projected eaves (A16).

Plate 6

◄Plate 6a: A medium-sized neo-Islamic-style house in Bahri al-Balad in Qena. The doorway located on the ground floor emphasizes the central bay of the house and is the entrance to *al-mandara*, which opens onto the main street. The top story is curved and has a rounded hole.

A17

► Plate 6b: The entire mashrabiya has small shutter windows, together with projected eaves and lower friezes (A17).

Plate 7

▲ Plate 7: Mashrabiya in Qena with two shutter windows in the front having projected eaves (A14). The doorway, which opens onto the main street, is the entrance to the reception unit, the *mandara*, which has one window at each side.

A14

Plate 8

▲ Plate 8: Façade of a house located in the main trading street in Qena. It consists of one central mashrabiya on the first floor, topped with an ordinary balcony on the second floor. The mashrabiya has three divided hinged lattice windows with projecting eaves (A18).

A18

Plate 9

A25

▲ Plate 9: Beautiful one-mashrabiya house in Beni Suef. There are two shutter windows, which are surrounded by fenestrated panels. The upper part of the mashrabiya has two half-rounded fenestrated panels. The projected eaves have upper and lower plant motifs (A25).

Plate 10

▲ Plate 10: A house with one mashrabiya in each façade resting on corbels, on the corner of al-Sayyida Hurriya and 'Umar streets in Beni Suef. The projected eaves have the characteristic double layers of plant motifs (A7 and A8).

A7

A8

Plate 11

◄ Plate 11: Façade of two houses in Qena. The first house has a closed-type mashrabiya with projected eaves (A19). The second house has an open-type mashrabiya with columns. Each house has one entrance leading to the *mandara*, which opens onto the street.

A19

Plate 12

◄Plate 12a: Open mashrabiya with columns in Qena. It has a single entrance, and two rooms in the *mandara*, which opens onto the street.

▶ Plate 12b: Mashrabiya with small shutter windows of movable louvered slates, which move up and down, and lower friezes (A12).

A12

Plate 13

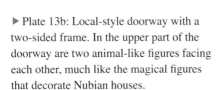

◄Plate 13a: A small house in Qena with an open mashrabiya with columns. It has one entrance.

▶ Plate 13b: Local-style doorway with a two-sided frame. In the upper part of the doorway are two animal-like figures facing each other, much like the magical figures that decorate Nubian houses.

Plate 14

◄Plate 14a: A medium-sized house on 41 Sidi Habib Street in Minya. It has two doorways, the first and largest being the family doorway, while the other one is small and simple and leads to an outer courtyard and on to the *mandara*.

▶ Plate 14b: Mashrabiya of glass screening characteristic of Minya. It has three vertical parts; the middle part has glass panes, while the upper part consists of star-plated wooden tracery. The bottom of the mashrabiya has star-plated ornamentation (C3). The mashrabiya is topped with projected eaves (A23).

C3

A23

E40

◄Plate 14c: Main doorway of a house displaying a combination of both Rumi-style stucco decoration (E48) and the European-style five-division doorway (E40).

E48

Plate 15

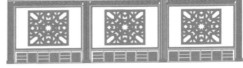

Plate 15a: A large house with glass screening on the corner of 67 Muhammad Badawi and Mahmud Abd al-Raziq streets in Minya.

C4

▶ Plate 15b: The lower part of the mashrabiya, with star-plated ornamentation, has been executed by means of small strips fixed with glue and nails (C4).

Plate 16

▶ Plate 16: House of the wealthy Dirbala family in Bahnasa (Minya Governorate). It exemplifies a reception unit, which greatly resembles the Rumi-style *salamlik* unit, with eaves of ornamented motifs (A1 and A3). The *mandara* block projecting beyond the façade level is above road level. It has a platform with a wrought-iron balustrade, supported by six wooden columns with ornamented arches.

A1

A3

Plate 17

▲ Plate 17: House located on the corner of al-Madrasa al-Amiriya and Sidi Habib streets in Minya. The entrance leading to the *mandara* is on al-Madrasa al-Amiriya Street. The *mandara* has a platform with four wooden columns.

Plate 18

▲ Plate 18a: A large house on the corner of 68 Muhammad Badawi and Mahmud Abd al-Raziq streets with a mashrabiya, the upper part of which is open.

C5

▶ Plate 18b: Mashrabiya with its open upper part in the form of two shallow arches. The base of the mashrabiya has four panels of star-plated ornamentation (C5).

Plate 19

◄Plate 19a: A small house on 20 Muhammad Shukri Street in Minya with one entrance and a *mandara* consisting of one room. This room has one window that looks out onto the main street.

C6

▶ Plate 19b: The upper part of the mashrabiya has two shallowly pierced wooden arches. The base of the mashrabiya rests upon corbels and has three ornamented panels (C6).

Plate 20

C7

◄Plate 20a: A small house in Biyr Abu Shamiya Street in Minya. Its mashrabiya, the upper part of which is open, is on the first floor, and an ordinary balcony with a wooden balustrade is on the second floor. The base of this mashrabiya has ornamented panels (C7).

▶ Plate 20b: One can observe a beautiful geometric type of arabesque in the upper parts of the vision area of this mashra-biya. The cover-like part above the arabesque has two friezes. The upper frieze has a double row of stalactites, while the lower frieze consists of abstract motifs.

Plate 21

▲ Plate 21: A medium-sized house in Suq al-Ghilal Street in Minya. The mashrabiya's cover-like upper part is in the shape of a wide arch of woodwork with plant motifs. The base of the mashrabiya has ornamented panels (C8).

C8

Plate 22

◀Plate 22a: A house in Biyr Abu Shamiya Street in Minya. It has two mashrabiyas in one of its façades, each with an upper opening. Another façade has one mashrabiya on the second floor.

▶ Plate 22b: The upper part of this mashrabiya has two shallow arches of pierced wood, while the vision area takes the form of panels of pierced wood (B70).

B70

Plate 23

◄Plate 23a: A large house in Muhammad Badawi Street in Minya with an upper-opening mashrabiya.

C9

► Plate 23b: The upper part of the mashrabiya is covered with glass panes. The base of the mashrabiya has three square panels with star-plated ornamentation (C9).

Plate 24

◄Plate 24a: Terrace at the southern façade of the Hayat al-Nufus Palace in Mallawi (Minya Governorate). The façade's projection and two recesses have pierced-wood screens.

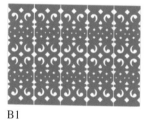

B1

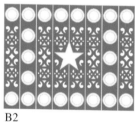

B2

▶ Plate 24b: Square panels screening the terrace's projections in the form of و shaped piercings, yielding an arabesque of the wider parts of plant-leaf shapes (B1 and B2).

Plate 25

▲ Plate 25: A small house in Mallawi (Minya Governorate) with an ordinary balcony. The two front panels that screen the balcony are made up of an arabesque of the wider parts of plant-leaf shapes (B3).

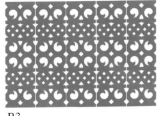

B3

Plate 26

▶ Plate 26: A medium-sized house in Mallawi (Minya Governorate). The gallery balcony screen is decorated with two types of arabesque ornamentation. The balcony on the first floor has an arabesque of very wide half-plant-leaf shapes (B11). However, the second floor is composed of a complete-plant-leaf arabesque (B9).

B11

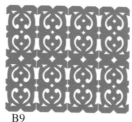

B9

Plate 27

▲ Plate 27: A medium-sized house in al-Shuhada Square in Tima (Sohag Governorate). On the top story is a trefoiled pediment with a hole. The pediment is emphasized by a projected cornice. The gallery balcony on the first floor has a high-level balustrade. The upper part of the balustrade is screened by an arabesque of small half-plant-leaf shapes (B4).

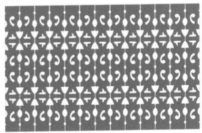

B4

Plate 28

▲Plate 28: A house in Mallawi (Minya Governorate). The balcony on the second story is screened by an arabesque of large half-plant-leaf shapes (B6).

B6

Plate 29

▲ Plate 29: A house in Mallawi (Minya Governorate) with one entrance and a *mandara* with a window. The high-level balustrades of the two ordinary balconies are screened by an arabesque of semi-complete plant leaves (B7).

B7

Plate 30

▲ Plate 30: A house in Manfalut (Asyut Governorate) with a closed large mashrabiya overlooking a commercial street. The ordinary balcony overlooks a small alley. The balcony has a screen decorated with an arabesque of complete-plant-leaf shapes with two lateral projections (B10).

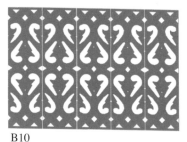

B10

Plate 31

▲ Plate 31: A medium-sized house in Tahta (Sohag Governorate). The upper part of the balcony's balustrade shows narrow, quintuple-plant-leaves arabesque (B13).

B13

Plate 32

▶Plate 32: A house in Girga (Sohag Governorate). The top-story façade shows a very simple curved pediment with a projected cornice and two piers, one on each of two corners of the building's façade. The piers have blunt pyramidal ends (D9). The upper part of the balcony's balustrade on the second story shows wide, quintuple-plant-leaves arabesque (B14). The balcony on the first story has a lattice-wood screen.

B14

Plate 33

▲ Plate 33: A small house in Girga (Sohag Governorate). The balcony's parapet on the first floor is in two equal halves. The screen of the upper half shows wide quintuple-plant-leaves arabesque (B16). The lower half shows long and narrow horizontal rhombuses, and also wide and short vertical rhombuses with projected bosses in the center.

B16

74

Plate 34

◀ Plate 34a: An elegant house in al-Hurriya Street in Girga (Sohag Governorate). The top story is in the Eclectic style with a local-style longitudinal opening (D3). Besides the two lateral bays of the ordinary balconies, there are also the central bays of the recessed gallery balconies.

B15

▶ Plate 34b: Ordinary balcony. The upper part of the parapet is screened with wide quintuple-plant-leaves arabesque (B15). The balcony's lower frieze is composed of arrow-head motifs (A5).

A5

Plate 35

▲ Plate 35a: A large house at the corner of al-Corniche and Hammam streets in Sohag.

▶ Plate 35b: The balustrade of the recessed gallery balcony is richly ornamented with wide quintuple-plant-leaves arabesque (B17).

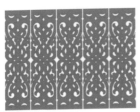

B17

◄ Plate 35c: A private Rumi-style entrance in the small Hammam Street in Sohag. The spandrel has garland motifs, and the entablature consists of two friezes. The upper frieze has dentiform ornamentation. The lower frieze, which is broader, has arches that are enclosed with star shapes (E47). The fanlight consists of short pear-shaped motifs (E6).

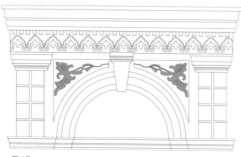

E47

E6

Plate 36

◀ Plate 36a: A medium-sized house in al-Maragha (Sohag Governorate), with two doorways and two mashrabiya-like balconies. The balconies are screened by means of three panels. The peripheries of the two rectangular panels have **V**-shaped arabesque ornamentations. The middle panel with lattice decoration in its center is surrounded by two strips of thin **V**-shaped arabesque ornamentations (B20).

B20

▶ Plate 36b: The simple doorway of this house serves as a private entrance, while the decorated doorway is the one leading to the *mandara*, which has two windows. The *mandara* doorway has rectangular fanlights (E44) and the usual five sections. The upper sections are made up of long rhombuses with projecting bosses.

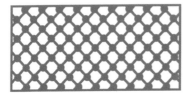

E44

Plate 37

Plate 37a: A house in the corner of al-Qaffas and al-Corniche streets in Sohag. It has two doorways, the visible one opening onto the main street, al-Corniche Street, which is the entrance to the *mandara*. The house has two recessed gallery balconies in its main facade, and a balcony with eaves at the corner of the building.

B28

Plate 37b: The balustrade of the first balcony consists of two parts; the screen of the upper part has **V**-shaped arabesque decorations (B28). The entire upper balustrade of the second-floor balcony has another type of **V**-shaped arabesque decoration (B18).

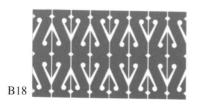

B18

Plate 38

◀Plate 38a: A medium-sized house in Abdin Street, off al-Gihad Street, in Tahta (Sohag Governorate). It has six balconies.

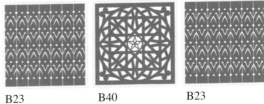

B23   B40   B23

▶Plate 38b: The balcony parapet has two parts. The upper part has three panels, the middle panel has a geometric-type arabesque, while the other two panels have **V**-shaped arabesque decorations (B23 and B40). The lower part of the parapet has local-type ornamentation.

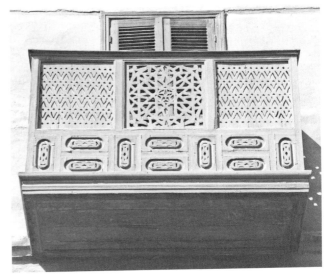

Plate 39

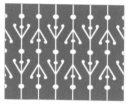

B21

▲ Plate 39: A small house in Tima (Sohag Governorate). The balconies have **V**-shaped arabesque piercings that yield wide arrowhead shapes (B21).

Plate 40

▲ Plate 40: A house in Qus (Qina Governorate).
The balcony's parapet has **V**-shaped arabesque
decorations (B25).

B25

Plate 41

◄Plate 41a: Eclectic-style house in Farid Sam'an Street, off Port Said Street in Tahta (Sohag Governorate).

B33   B35   B33

▼Plate 41b: Projected gallery balcony of plant-type arabesque decoration (B33 and B35).

Plate 42

▲ Plate 42a: Eclectic-style house in 'Anbar Street, off al-Gihad Street, in Tahta (Sohag Governorate), with projected-type gallery balconies.

▲ Plate 42b: The upper part of the balconies' balustrades are divided into five panels that have various types of plant and geometric arabesque decoration (B32, B34, B38, B41).

B32   B34   B41   B34   B32

B34   B38   B41   B38   B34

Plate 43

Plate 43a: A medium-sized house on 16 Abdin Street, off al-Gihad Street, in Tahta (Sohag Governorate). The upper part of the balustrade consists of various panels of geometric and plant-type arabesque ornamentation (B19, B36, B48) The lower part of the balcony on the first story displays the local type of short (figure 1) and long ornamentation (figure 2).

B36 B19 B36 B48

Plate 44

◄Plate 44a: Wealthy family house in Dayrut al-Sharif (Asyut Governorate) with two doorways. The first doorway has stucco decoration all over and is the entrance to a *mandara* with three windows, while the other one is the private doorway. The house's main façade displays a combination of mashrabiya with four columns and three arches and a recessed gallery balcony.

B37

B5

▶ Plate 44b: The lower part of the mashrabiya is screened with a geometric type of arabesque (B37), while the top floor is screened by waw-shaped و arabesque (B5).

Plate 45

B42

▲ Plate 45: A house in George al-'Ibidi Street, off Port Said Street, in Tahta (Sohag Governorate). The balustrade of the recessed gallery balcony is composed of a square panel in the middle of star-plate ornamentation, while the other two, rectangular, panels are made up of manifold styles of arabesque (B42).

Plate 46

◀Plate 46a: A house in Port Said Street in Asyut, belonging to Khashaba Pasha. It has one entrance, which leads to a *mandara* composed of a gallery balcony (now closed by bricks) and a one-window room. The house has a combination of an open mashrabiya with two columns and a recessed-type gallery balcony.

▼Plate 46b: The lower part of the balcony's balustrade is decorated with manifold arabesque ornamentations. One can observe that the two irregular, separate shapes in the lower part of the screen seem like an arch in the upper part of the screen seams (B43).

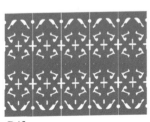

B43

Plate 47

B44

▲ Plate 44: A medium-sized house in al-Rahba Street, off Port Said Street, in Asyut. The top story is made up of a high-level wall. The lower parts of the balconies are screened with manifold-type arabesque (B44), while the upper parts (the vision areas) feature wide arches.

Plate 48

▲ Plate 48: A large house belonging to the
wealthy Mu'awwad family in Dayrut al-Sharif
(Asyut Governorate). The two doorways on the
ground floor are the entrances to the two reception areas (probably one each for male and
female guests); each *mandara* has two windows. The entrances are made of three steps,
and a platform, opening onto the outer courtyard. The first floor has two recessed gallery
balconies, their screens showing manifold
arabesque decorations (B45).

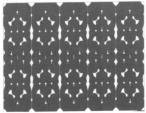

B45

Plate 49

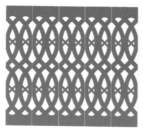

B47

▲ Plate 49: A house in al-Gaysh Street in Tima (Sohag Governorate) founded in 1932. The top story is in the Eclectic style (D2). The doorway is in wrought iron and leads to the outer courtyard. The central bay is composed of projected gallery balconies with two columns, while the lateral bay contains recessed gallery balconies. Both types of balconies are screened by fret-type arabesque (B47).

Plate 50

▲ Plate 50a: A house belonging to al-Sheikh al-Maraghi in al-Maragha (Sohag Governorate). It has two entrances. The visible *mandara* entrance, which opens onto the street, leads to two reception areas, each with two windows. The house has two recessed gallery balconies.

▲ Plate 50b: The upper part of the first-floor balcony is made up of a longitudinal opening screen. Its lower part has local-type ornamentation. The second-floor balcony has a screen of mixed types of ornamentation (B30, B54). The top floor has another type of longitudinal screen (B56).

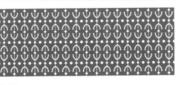

B54

B30

B54

B56

Plate 51

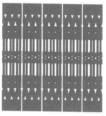

B57

▲ Plate 51: A medium-size house in Qena. The screens on both the first and second floors have longitudinally shaped openings (B57). The top story of the adjacent house has very high walls with pyramidal pediments and two piers, one at each corner.

Plate 52

◄Plate 49: A house in
Ahmad Mahir Street in
Tima (Sohag Governorate).
It has two doorways; the
smaller is the private one,
and the larger is the *mandara* entrance. The first
story has a recessed gallery
balcony with a very high
screen. The screen consists
of three parts, reflecting a
gradual change of screen-
ing (B59). The top story
has a longitudinal opening
screen (B58).

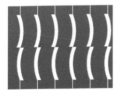

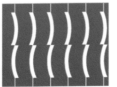

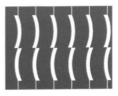

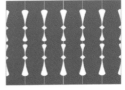

B59

B58

Plate 53

◀Plate 53: A house in Ahmad Mahir Street in Tima (Sohag Governorate). It has two similar doorways, one private, the other leading to the *mandara* entrance. The first story has two high-level balconies. The base of the parapet consists of three parts, each of which have square panel decorations (C10).

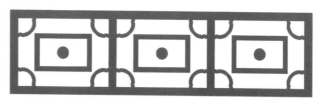

C10

Plate 54

C11

◀Plate 54a: A house on the corner of Rifa'a and al-Gumhuriya streets in Tima (Sohag Governorate). The decoration of the lower part of the balcony's parapet is done in the local style (C11).

▶Plate 54b: Eclectic-style doorway with a wide frame and projected pediment. There is a frieze of dentiform ornamentation between fanlight and door-leaf area. The plate-band area shows an engraved figure.

Plate (86)

Plate 55

◀Plate 55a: A house at 5 al-Sagha Street in Nagʻ Hammadi (Qena Governorate). There are two balconies on the first floor. The upper parts of both parapets are screened by differently shaped panels of lattice wood. The second floor has a central recessed gallery balcony.

▶Plate 55b: Upper-floor balcony with a projected balustrade; its lower surface is decorated with a painting showing a natural scene.

Plate 56

▲ Plate 56: An apartment building on 26th July Street in Asyut, built in 1926. The corner has a long high-level parapet completely covered with wooden sheets.

Plate 57

▲ Plate 57a: A house belonging to
Mustafa Qurashi, the house's founder
and member of a wealthy family in
Dayrut al-Mahatta (Asyut governorate).

C12

▶ Plate 57b: Balcony with a high parapet. The upper half of the balcony has
pierced-wood windows (C12).

Plate 58

▲ Plate 58: A medium-sized house at 112 al-Mithaq Street in Asyut. The upper third of the balconies are screened with pyriform-shaped ornamentation (B62).

B62

Plate 59

▲ Plate 59: A small house at 86 al-Mithaq Street in Asyut. It has one doorway and a *mandara* with one window. The second-story balcony is screened with pyriform-shaped ornamentation (B63).

B63

Plate 60

▲ Plate 60: A medium-sized house on al-Shishtawi Alley, off Ahmad 'Arabi Street, in Beni Suef. The balcony has pierced-wood ornamentations in the form of bell-shaped roses (B61).

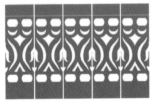

B61

Plate 61

B31

▲ Plate 61: A small-scale house in Ahmed 'Urabi Street in Beni Suef. The balcony is screened with oval-shaped pierced wood ornamentation (B31).

Plate 62

B71

▲ Plate 62: A medium-size house in Beni Suef. The upper story has two tower-like projections, one at each corner of the building. The top story has a high-level wall with longitudinal recesses and projections. The upper part of the tower is screened with half-rounded and rectangular fenestrations (B71).

Plate 63

▶ Plate 63: The top story of a house in Biyr Abu Shamiya in Minya. It has a high-level wooden screen, which is indeed higher than the adjacent house.

Plate 64

▲ Plate 61a: House belonging to Muhammad Pasha Qurashi (built in the 1920s) in Dayrut al-Mahatta (Asyut Governorate). The façade has a mashrabiya-like projected gallery balcony. The *mandara* (or *salam-lik*) on the ground floor has four steps leading down to the house's outer courtyard. The house has a high-level top story with a longitudinal opening. The pediment is topped by a large crescent (D6).

◄ Plate 61b: The middle and lower parts of the mashrabiya are screened with pierced-wood orna-mentation (B53).

B53

Plate 65

▶ Plate 65: A local-style top story of a small house in al-Markaz Street in Qena. The pediment of the top story has stucco decorations, and is topped by an eagle with outstretched wings. The piers at the corners of the building look like two obelisks (D5). The gallery balcony has a lower frieze with ornamentation (A11).

A11

Plate 66

◄Plate 66: A local-style top story of a small house in al-Markaz Street in Qena. The stepped pediment is decorated with a projected cornice (D8).

D8

Plate 67

▶Plate 67: A local-style top story of small houses on 26 July Street in Asyut. It shows two shapes of pediment, which are demarcated by projected cornices (D10, D11).

D10   D11

Plate 68

▲ Plate 68: A medium-sized house in Qena with a curved pediment. The wall of the top story has longitudinal openings (D4).

D4

Plate 69

▲ Plate 69a: A large Rumi-style house in al-Sit Hurriya Street in Beni Suef, built in AH 1304/1886 CE, as is written in the hub of the fanlight.

▶ Plate 69b: Doorway with one leaf. The fanlight has long pyriform motifs in wrought iron (E10). The entablature has a wide projected frieze. The upper parts of the pilasters have an ornamented crown.

E10

Plate 70

◀ Plate 70: A Rumi-style doorway on al-Bashmuhandis Street, off al-Corniche Street, in Sohag. All of the entablature, the archivolt, the upper part of the pilasters, and also the lintel of the door display stalactites. The spandrels have *jift* and *mima* motifs (E46). The fanlight has rounded and short pyriform motifs in wrought iron (E5).

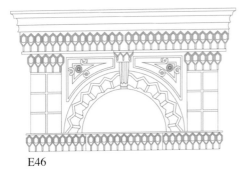

E46

E5

Plate 71

▲ Plate 71: Eclectic-style doorway in Tahta (Sohag Governorate) with unique scroll motifs of wrought iron in three rows (E19).

E19

Plate 72

◄ Plate 72: Local-style
doorway of a small house in
Tahta (Sohag Governorate).
The fanlight is surrounded
by a wooden frame with
dentiform ornamentations.
The wrought iron of the fanlight shows pyriform and
crescent motifs (E9).

E9

Plate 73

▶Plate 73: Eclectic-style doorway in Ahmad Mahir Street in Tima (Sohag Governorate). The two-leaf door and the six-sided fanlight are surrounded by a wooden frame. The fanlight has pyriform motifs (E32), and the various sections of the door's leaves have engraved ornamentations.

E32

Plate 74

◄Plate 74: Eclectic-style doorway on 26 al-Tahrir Street, off Muhammad Ali Makarm Street, in Asyut. The two-leaf door and the fanlight (E34) are surrounded by a wooden frame of engraved ornamentations. The plate-band area contains a scene showing an angel with outstretched wings. Both the lower section and the door's threshold have plant-motif ornamentations.

E34

Plate 75

▲ Plate 75: Traditional longitudinal openings
of the top floor of a house in al-Qasr.

Plate 76

▲ Plate 76: Main doorway of a simple arch leading to the reception unit *(madyafa)* of a house in al-Qasr (Dakhla Oasis). The wooden lintel contains inscriptions in double rows.

Plate 77

▲ Plate 77: Wooden lintel of a door to a house in al-Qasr. It belongs to the prince Zulfiqar Bey. The house dates back to AH 1082/1672 CE, according to an engraving on the door lintel.

Plate 78

◄Plate 78a: Main doorway to a house in al-Qasr. It has a recessed entrance with an arch. This entrance is decorated with various arrangements of mud bricks.

▼Plate 78b: This doorway's lintel has a decorated boss at each side. The whole lintel is surrounded by twists (F1).

F1

Plate 79

Plate 79a: The *madyafa* doorway of the al-Hagg Muhammad Shams al-Din al-Qurashi family in al-Qasr. The house dates back to AH 1083/CE 1673. The doorway arch is decorated mainly with *mangur* bricks in stepped motifs.

Plate 79b: Lintel of a house of the Qurashi family containing inscriptions that are displayed in two rows. This lintel has two large decorated bosses, one at each side (F2).

F2

Plate 80

▲ Plate 80: Doorway of a house in Qus (Qena Governorate). Its
lintel has six inscription areas and five decorated bosses (F5).

F5

Plate 81

▲ Plate 81: Lintel of a house in Qus (Qena Governorate), the right part of which is damaged. It is supposed to have six inscription areas and five decorated bosses (F6).

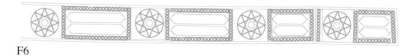

F6

Plate 82

▲ Plate 82: A house in Qena, decorated with *mangur* bricks.

APPENDICES OF
DECORATIVE ELEMENTS

APPENDIX A

Wooden Friezes of Mashrabiya Eaves

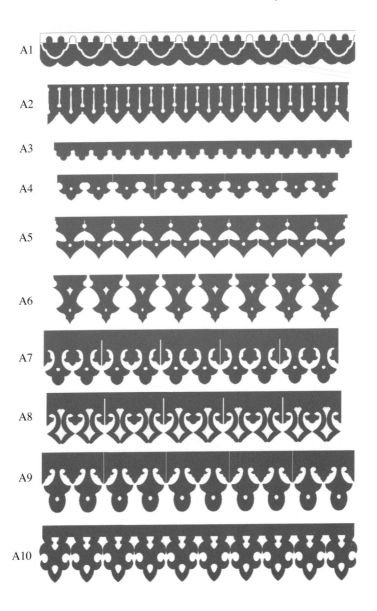

A1

A2

A3

A4

A5

A6

A7

A8

A9

A10

A11

A12

A13

A14

A15

A16

A17

A18

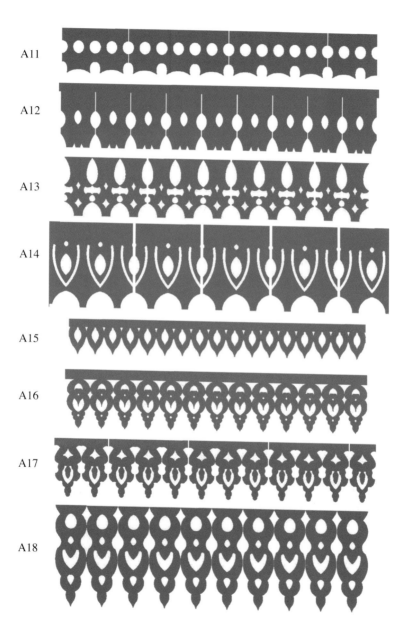

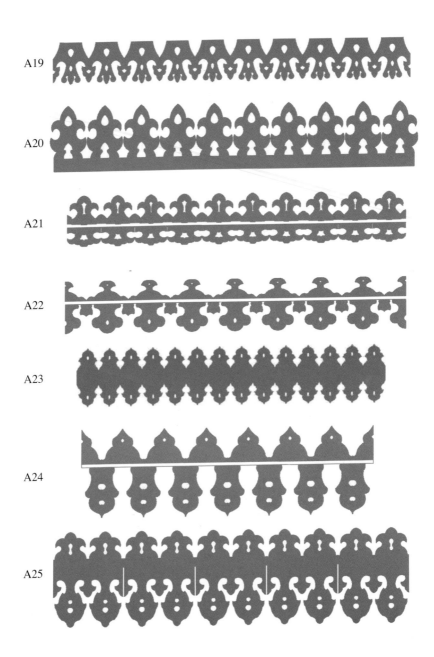

A19

A20

A21

A22

A23

A24

A25

APPENDIX B

Wooden Screens

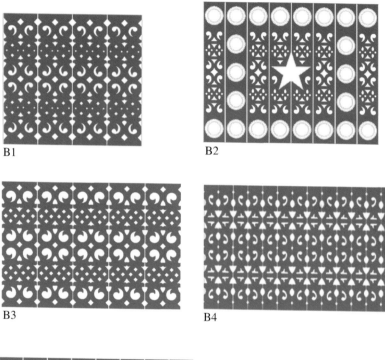

B1

B2

B3

B4

B5

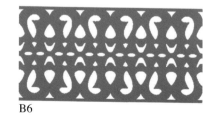

B6

B7

B8

B9

B10

B11

B12

B13

B14

B15

B16

B17

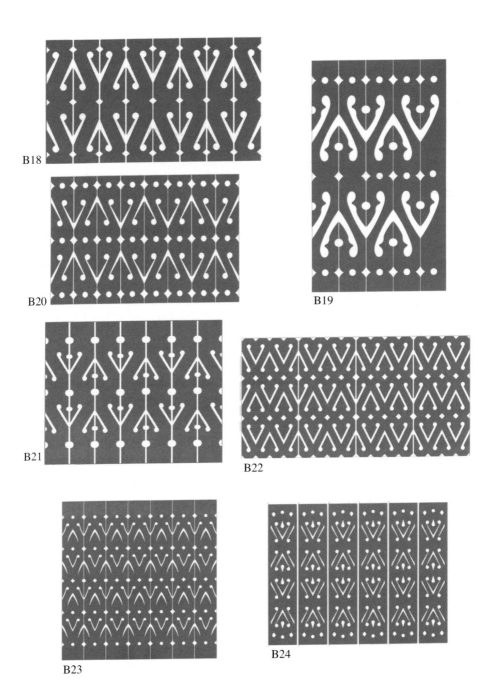

B18

B20

B19

B21

B22

B23

B24

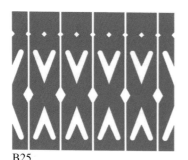

B25

B26

B27

B28

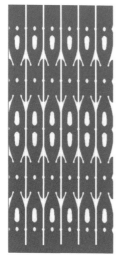

B29

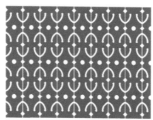

B30

B31

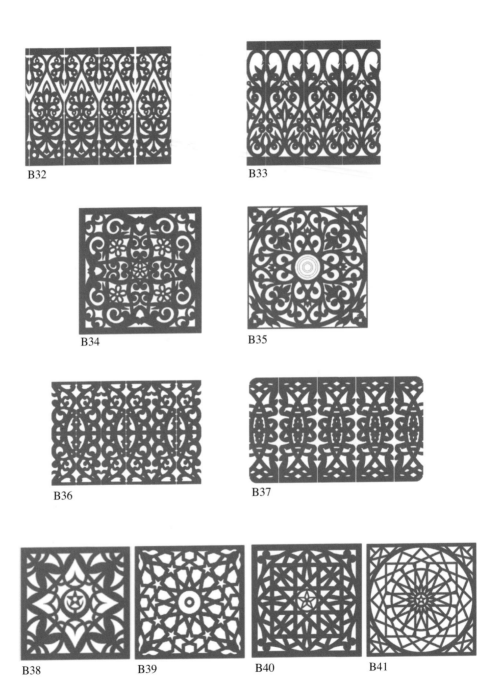

B32

B33

B34

B35

B36

B37

B38

B39

B40

B41

B42

B43

B44

B45

B46

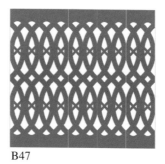

B47

B48

B49

B50

B51

B52

B53

B54

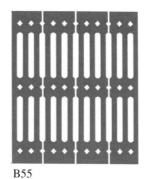

B55

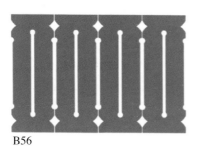

B56

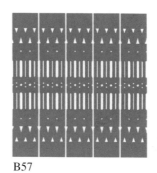

B57

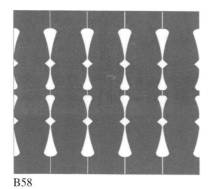

B58

B59

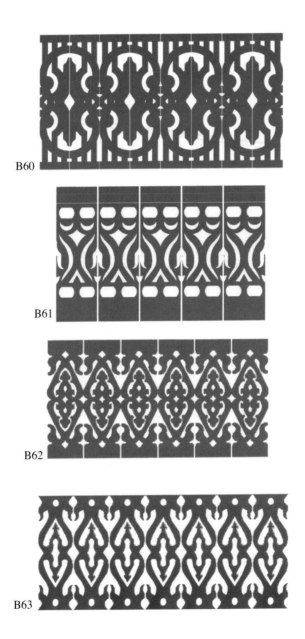

B60

B61

B62

B63

B64

B65

B66

B67

B68

B69

B70

B71

APPENDIX C

Wooden Ornamentation

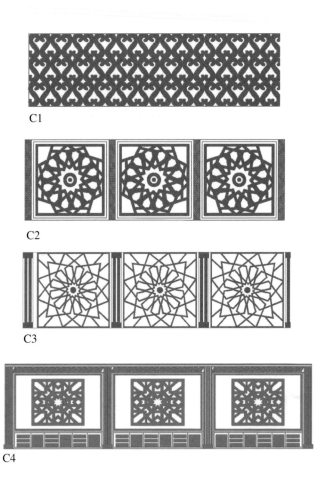

C1

C2

C3

C4

C5

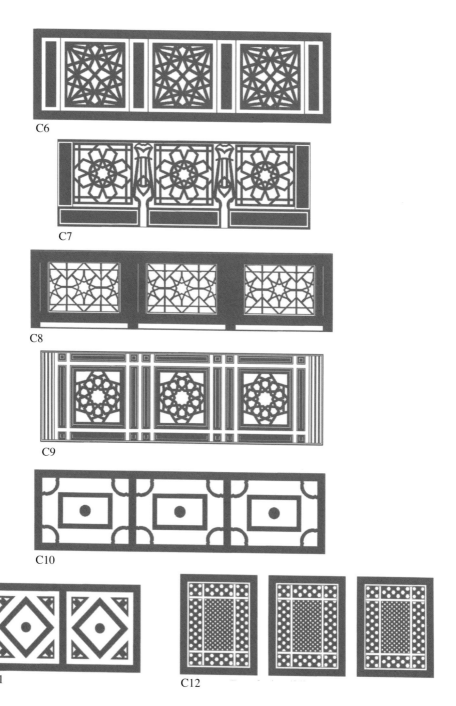

C6

C7

C8

C9

C10

C11

C12

APPENDIX D

Pediments and Rooflines

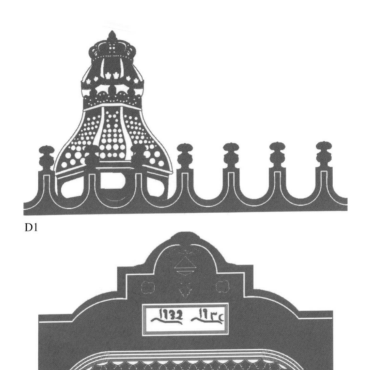

D1

D2

D3

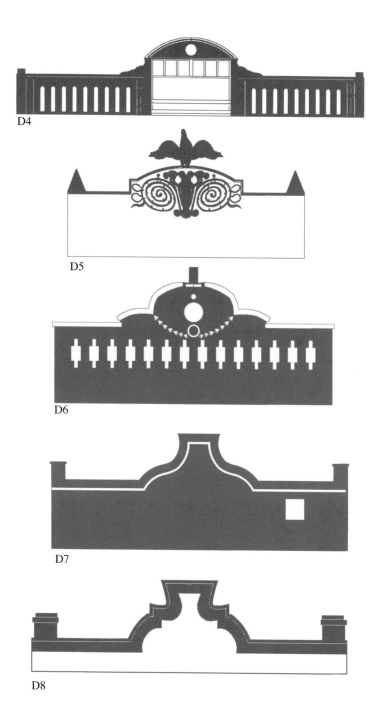

D4

D5

D6

D7

D8

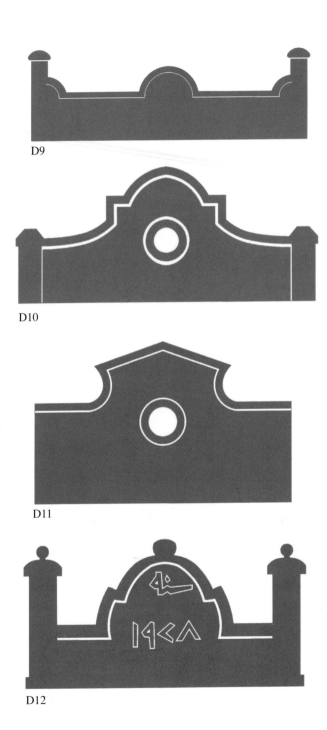

D9

D10

D11

D12

APPENDIX E

Fanlights and
Upper Parts of Doorways

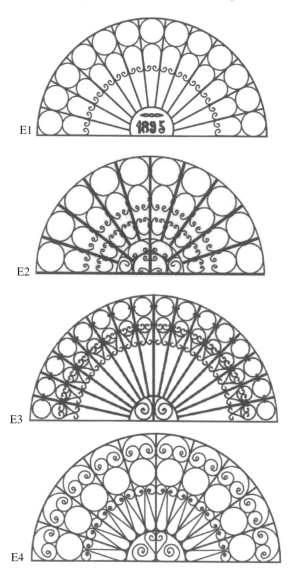

E1

E2

E3

E4

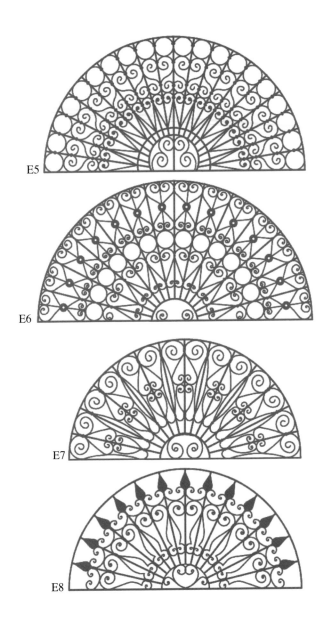

E5

E6

E7

E8

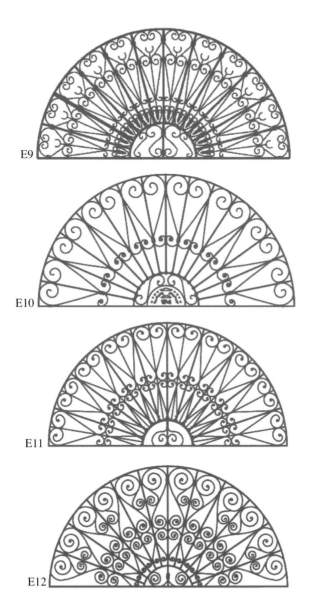

E9

E10

E11

E12

E13

E14

E15

E16

E17

E18

E19

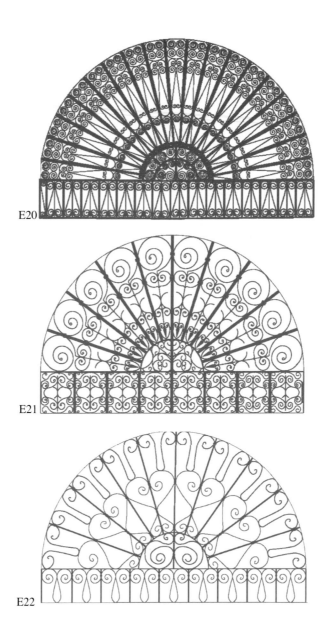

E20

E21

E22

E23

E24

E25

E26

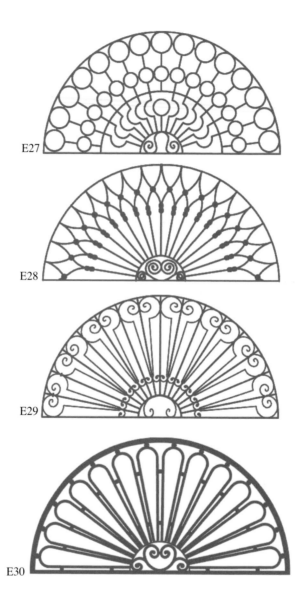

E27

E28

E29

E30

E31

E32

E33

E34

E35

E36

E37

E38

E39

E40

E41

E42

E43

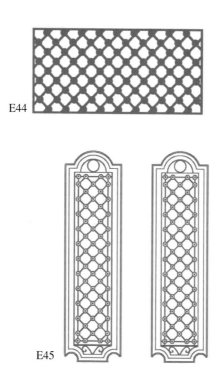

E44

E45

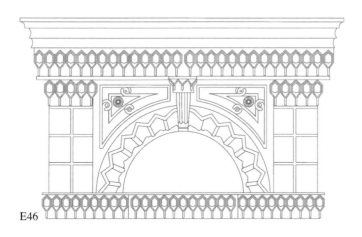

E46

E47

E48

APPENDIX F

Lintels

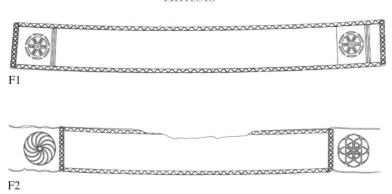

F1

F2

F3

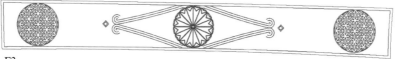

F4

F5

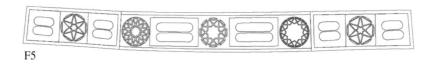

F6

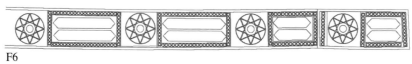

GLOSSARY

durqa'a: a square or rectangular area behind a doorway; it has a side passage that leads to the main courtyard (from the Bahri Mamluk period)

jift: widespread Islamic decorative units of two parallel bars ending in either a *mima* (Islamic decoration taking the circular shape of the Arabic letter *mim*) or a scissor motif

lime plastering: a method of plastering that relies on the use of limestone (calcium carbonate); after being burnt, it transforms into calcium oxide; after the addition of water, it becomes calcium hydroxide; by adding sodium chloride, it becomes limewater, which contains dissolved calcium salts, which are used in white plaster. Different colors can be added to the limewater.

mandara, or *madyafa*: a reception hall

mangur: a type of brick made from special mud clay capable of enduring high temperatures and characterized by its solidness, making it suitable for building and decoration. The preparation of *mangur* bricks can go through several stages, during which it can take on a variety of colors, including black and brown.

ma'qali: wood decorations consisting of vertical and horizontal rectangular pieces enclosed within a square piece in the center.

salamlik: a reception unit in Rumi-style architecture, used for male guests.

takhtabush: a reception unit which opens on to the inner courtyard facing north (from the Ottoman period)